How to Get Rid of "it"

Before "it" Gets Rid of You

Healing and Deliverance from Personality Disorders

A Practical Self-Help Guide to Spiritual and Personal Growth

*A series of easy spiritual exercises, interactive tools,
And step-by-step instructions to receive
Freedom from bondage
And experience spiritual healing and deliverance*

Volume Three

ISBN-13: 978-1986165679

ISBN-10: 1986165671

How to Get Rid of "it"

Before "it" Gets Rid of You

Healing and Deliverance from Personality Disorders

A Practical Self-Help Guide to Spiritual and Personal Growth

A series of easy spiritual exercises, interactive tools,
And step-by-step instructions to receive
Freedom from bondage
And experience spiritual healing and deliverance

Volume Three

Compilations of Works
By
Dr. Paulette Douglas

DEDICATION

**This book is dedicated to my Loving, Supportive, Mother,
The late Dr. Bernice Woods**

**All my life, my mother has inspired me to be the Women that God has ordained me to be
and to continue to minister to God's people and to make full proof of my ministry**

CONTENT

How to Get Rid of "it", Before "it" Gets Rid of You

PREFACE

How to Get Rid of "it", Before "it" Gets Rid of You is a Deliverance and Spiritual Warfare Manual compiled by Dr. Paulette Douglas which is worth reading and re-reading more than once, in order to empower the reader when confronting personal crisis and trials. Dr. Paulette Douglas has compiled many practical, spiritual books bringing light to the evil that exists. She brings the deliverance ministry to the forefront, explaining how each and every believer can counteract evil and the devil. Not many believers understand the concept of the Holy Spirit and that we are all called to fight against the devil, our enemy. Dr. Paulette Douglas presents scriptural background and Bible passages from the old and new testaments, as well as prayers to share with the reader that each of us is called to resist and fight against the devil with the power of the Holy Spirit. Dr. Paulette Douglas refers to this as the deliverance ministry and explains this is one of the privileges all believers have at our disposal.

This background scripture material is necessary as many readers may be unfamiliar with these spiritual concepts. The main focus on the book is to be a manual; or one stop guide to show the reader what the bible has to say about deliverance as well as to expose the works and deceptions of the devil as well. The cover itself might seem an actual handbook- yet this book is truly a manual for deliverance. This exhaustive book contains too much information to be digested in a single, quick reading. The words contained are life changing. While some traditional readers and those in organized religion may find this book difficult to believe and a bit theatrical, a close-minded attitude is exactly what the devil wants in order to operate.

It is important to keep in mind the charismatic background of Dr. Paulette Douglas is based on the belief of the real workings of the Holy Spirit and the literal belief in modern day spiritual gifts such as tongues and healing. Much of the book is an invaluable resource where Dr. Douglas has taken scriptural truths and prayers and relates them to the modern-day believer to use and apply when facing any trial or work from the enemy. The scriptural references will empower any reader with a quick resource of how to respond in faith to any difficulty- large and small. It is a spiritual self-help book in the fact that it will allow the reader the tools to look within himself/her-self and identify any areas or issues where Satan has his foothold. Not only that it tells the reader how to face and address these issues! For those who are at a loss of how to begin to approach their spiritual problems there are a number of sample prayers applicable to any number of situations. The reader will get the impression as if this book was written for his or her own situation. This is a book to meditate on and use- and is not intended to collect dust on a book shelf. There are eleven sequels to this handbook which address many other issues that just might cover your "it".

In this twelve-book series, How to Get Rid of "it" Before "it" gets Rid of You we discuss evil spirits and how they operate:
1. The Apostolic anointing and ministry
2. How demons enter and oppress people
3. Curses and how to deal with them
4. Breaking bondages
5. Casting out spirits

6. Healing the wounded heart
7. Ungodly beliefs
8. Ministering to people
9. House cleansing
10. Discerning of spirits

In this volume, we deal with the root causes of the "it' of personality disorders and How to get rid of the "it" of personality disorders before it gets rid of you. Personality disorders is something that plagues many people today, whether your personality disorders cause an addiction to food, sex, drugs, alcohol, smoking, spending, masturbation, porn, etc. Some inexperienced deliverance ministers might go after a spirit of personality disorders, which may bring freedom, but often, it doesn't bring lasting freedom. Many times, there is a root that needs to be pulled up, alongside casting out any residing spirits that are holding the person in bondage to the personality disorders. Getting to the root of the personality disorders is the key to bringing a person lasting genuine freedom. I am going to address the most common roots to personality disorders, and hopefully give you an idea of how this bondage works so that you can minister lasting freedom to this type of bondage.

INTRODUCTION

"It Is Finished"
The Words of Victory

"When Jesus therefore had received the vinegar, he said, "It is finished.""—John 19:30
Words of triumph. In His words, "My God, my God, why hast thou forsaken me?" we heard the
Savior's cry of desolation. In His words, "I thirst" we listened to His cry of lamentation. Now
there falls upon our ears His cry of jubilation— "It is finished." From the words of the victim we
turn now to the words of the Victor. The Cross of Christ has two great sides to it: it showed the
profound depths of His humiliation, but it also marked the goal of the Incarnation, and further, it
told the consummation of His mission, and it forms the basis of our salvation.

It is finished." What is found in these three words, "It is finished" is wrapped up the Gospel of
God. In these words, contained the ground of the believer's assurance. In those words, is
discovered the sum of all joy, and the very spirit of all divine consolation. Every" it" that we
could ever encounter in our lives was dealt with on the cross therefore; we have the victory
through Jesus Christ over any and every "it".

"It is finished." This was not the despairing cry of a helpless martyr. It was not an expression of
satisfaction that the termination of His sufferings was now reached. It was not the last gasp of a
worn-out life. No, rather was it the declaration on the part of the divine Redeemer that all for
which He came from heaven to earth to do, was now done; that all that was needed to reveal the
full character of God had now been accomplished; that all that was required by the Law before
sinners could be saved, had now been performed—that the full price of our redemption was now
paid.

"It is finished." The great purpose of God in the history of man was now accomplished—from
the beginning, God's purpose has always been one and indivisible. It had been declared to men
in numerous ways: in symbol and type, by mysterious hints and by plain intimations, through
Messianic prediction and through didactic declaration. That purpose of God may be summarized
thus: to display His grace in the creating of children in His own image and glory. And at the
Cross the foundation was laid which was to make this possible and actual.

"It is finished." What was finished? The answer to this question is a very full one, though many
excellent expositors have sought to limit the scope of these words and to confine them strictly to
a single application. We are told it was the prophecies concerning the sufferings of Jesus which
were finished, and that He referred only to this. It is readily granted that the immediate reference
was to the Messianic predictions, yet we think there are good and sufficient reasons for not
confining our Lord's words here to them. Yea, to us it seems certain that Christ referred specially
to His sacrificial work, for all Scripture concerning His suffering and shame was not yet fulfilled.
There remained the dismissal of His spirit into the hands of the Father (Psa 31:5); there remained
the "piercing" with the spear (Zec 12:10: and note that the word used in Psalm 22:16 for the
piercing of His hands and feet—the act of crucifixion—is a different one); there still remained

the preserving of His bones unbroken (Psa 34:20), and the burial in the rich man's grave (Isa 53:9).

"It is finished." What was finished? We answer His sacrificial work. It is true there yet remained the act of death itself, which was necessary for the making of atonement. But, as is so often the case here in John's Gospel wherein our text is found (cf. Joh 12:23, 31; 13:31; 16:5; 17:4), the Lord here speaks of the completion of His work. Moreover, it must be remembered that the three hours darkness was already past, the awful cup had already been drained, His precious blood had already been shed, the outpoured wrath of God had already been endured; and these are the primary elements in the making of propitiation. The sacrificial work of Jesus, then, was completed, excepting only the act of death which followed immediately. But, as we shall see, the completing of the sacrificial work made an end of several things.

"It is finished."
1. Here we see the accomplished fulfillment of all the prophecies which had been written of Him here He should die. This is the immediate thought of the context: "When Jesus therefore had received the vinegar, He said, It is finished" (John 19:30). Centuries beforehand, the prophets of God had described step by step the humiliation and suffering which the coming Savior should undergo. One by one these had been fulfilled, wonderfully fulfilled, fulfilled to the very letter. Had prophecy declared that He should be the "woman's seed" (Gen 3:15), then He was "born of a woman" (Gal 4:4). Had prophecy announced that His mother should be a "virgin" (Isa 7:14), then was it literally fulfilled (Mat 1:18). Had prophecy revealed that He should be of the seed of Abraham (Gen 22:18), then mark its fulfillment (Mat 1:1). Had prophecy made it known that He

Prophecy said that He should be named before He was born (Isa 49:1), then so it came to pass (Luke 1:30-31). Had prophecy foretold that He should be born in Bethlehem of Judea (Mic 5:2), then mark how this very village was His birthplace. Had prophecy forewarned that His birth should entail sorrowing for others (Jer 31:15), then behold its tragic fulfillment (Mat 2:14-18). Had prophecy foreshown that the Messiah should appear before the scepter of tribal ascendancy had departed from Judah (Gen 49:10), then so He did, for though the ten tribes were in captivity, Judah was still in the land at the time of His advent. Had prophecy referred to the flight into Egypt and the subsequent return into Palestine, (Hose 11:1 and cf. Isa 49:3, 6), then so it came to pass (Mat 2:1415).

Prophecy made mention of one going before Christ to make ready His way (Mal 3:1), then see its fulfillment in the person of John the Baptist. Had prophecy made it known that at the Messiah's appearing "the eyes of the blind shall be opened, and the ears of the deaf shall be unstopped, then shall the lame man leap as a hart, and the tongue of the dumb sing" (Isa 35:56), then read through the four Gospels and see how blessedly this proved true. Had prophecy spoken of Him as "poor and needy" (Psa 40:17, see beginning of Psalm), then behold Him not having where to lay His head. Had prophecy intimated that He should speak in "parables" (Psa 78:2), then such was frequently His method of teaching. Had prophecy depicted Him stilling the tempest (Psa 107:29), then this is exactly what He did. Had prophecy heralded His "triumphal entry" into Jerusalem (Zec 9:9), then so it came to pass!

Prophecy announced that His person should be despised (Isa 53:3), that He should be rejected by the Jews (Isa 8:14), that He should be "hated without a cause" (Psa 69:4), then sad to say, such was precisely the case. Had prophecy painted the whole picture of His degradation and crucifixion, then was it vividly reproduced. There had been the betrayal by a familiar friend, the forsaking by His disciples, the being led to the slaughter, the being taken to judgment, the appearing of false witnesses against Him, the refusal on His part to make defense, the establishing of His innocence, the unjust condemnation, the sentence of capital punishment passed upon Him, the literal piercing of His hands and feet, the being numbered with transgressors, the mockery of the crowd, the casting lots for His garments—all predicted centuries beforehand, and all fulfilled to the very letter. The last prophecy of all which remained here He committed His Spirit into the hands of His Father, had now been fulfilled. He cried "I thirst," and after the tendering of the vinegar and gall, all was now "accomplished"; and as the Lord Jesus reviewed the entire scope of the prophetic Word and saw its full realization, He cried,

"It is finished"!
It only remains for us to point out that as there was a complete set of prophecies which had to do with the first advent of Jesus, so also is there a complete set of prophecies which have to do with His second advent—the latter as definite, as personal, and as comprehensive in their scope as the former. As then we see the actual fulfillment of those which had to do with His first coming to the earth, we may look forward with absolute confidence and assurance to the fulfillment of those which have to do with His second coming. And, as we have seen that the former set of prophecies were fulfilled literally and personally, so also must we expect the latter set to be. To grant the literal fulfillment of the former, and then to seek to spiritualize and symbolize the latter, is not only grossly inconsistent and illogical, but is highly injurious to us and deeply dishonoring to God and to His Word.

"It is finished."
2. Here we see the completion of His sufferings. But what tongue or pen can describe the sufferings of Jesus? The anguish, physical, mental, and spiritual, which He endured! Appropriately was He designated "the man of sorrows": suffering at the hands of men, at the hands of Satan, and at the hands of God. Pain inflicted upon Him by enemies and friends alike. From the beginning He walked the shadows which the Cross cast His path. "I am afflicted and ready to die from my youth up" (Psa 88:15). What a light this throws on His earlier years! Who can say how much is contained in those words? For us, an impenetrable veil is cast over the future; none of us knows what a day may bring forth.

But Jesus knew the end from the beginning! One has only to read through the Gospels to learn how the awful Cross was ever before Him. At the marriage-feast of Cana, where all was gladness and merriment, He makes solemn reference to "his hour" not yet come. When Nicodemus interviewed Him at night, the Savior referred to the "lifting up of the Son of man." When James and John came to request from Him the two places of honor in His coming kingdom, He made mention of the "cup" which He had to drink, and of the "baptism" wherewith He must be baptized. When Peter confessed that He was the Christ, the Son of the living God, He turned to His disciples and began to show unto them "how that he must go unto Jerusalem, and suffer many things of the elders and chief priests and scribes, and be killed, and be raised again the third day" (Mat 16:21). When Moses and Elijah stood with Him on the Mount of Transfiguration, it was to speak of "his decease which he should accomplish at Jerusalem" (Luke 9:31).

If it is true we are quite unable to estimate the sufferings of Christ due to the anticipation of the Cross, still less can we fathom the dread reality itself. The physical sufferings were excruciating, but even this was as nothing compared with His anguish of soul. To a consideration of these sufferings we have already devoted several paragraphs in previous chapters, yet we make no apology in turning to them again. We cannot contemplate too often what Jesus endured to secure our salvation. The better we are acquainted with His sufferings, and the more frequently we meditate thereon, the warmer will be our love and the deeper our gratitude.
At last the closing hours have come. There had been the terrible experience in Gethsemane followed by the appearing before Caiaphas, before Pilate, before Herod, and back again before Pilate. There had been the scourging and mocking by the brutal soldiers; the journey to Calvary; the fastening of His hands and feet to the cruel tree. There had been the reviling of the priests, the crowd, and the two thieves crucified with Him.

There had been the awful cloud that hid from the Father's face, which wrung from Him the bitter cry, "My God, my God, why hast thou forsaken me?" There had been the parched lips which drew from Him the exclamation "I thirst." There had been the fearful conflict with the power of darkness as the serpent "bruised" His heel. But now the suffering is ended. The Lord has bruised Him; man, and Devil have done their worst. The cup has been drained. The awful storm of God's wrath has spent itself. The darkness is ended. The sword of divine justice is done. The wages of sin have been paid. The prophecies of His sufferings are all fulfilled. The Cross has been "endured." Divine holiness has been fully satisfied (Isa 53:11). With a cry of triumph—a loud cry, a cry which reverberated throughout the entire universe—Jesus exclaims, "It is finished." The shame, the suffering and agony, are past. Never again shall He experience pain. Never again shall He endure the contradiction of sinners against Himself. Never again shall He be in the hands of Satan. Never again shall the light of God's countenance be hidden from Him. Blessed be God, all that is finished! "It is finished."

Jesus is concerned in the work of Redemption: He was the One who came here to die for sinners. He is the One who now gives spiritual illumination and understanding, and guides into the truth. Before the Lord Jesus came to this earth, a definite work was committed to Him. In the volume of the book it was written of Him, and He came to do the recorded will of God. Even as a boy of twelve the "Father's business" was before His heart and occupied His attention. Again, in John 5:36 we find Him saying, "But I have greater witness than that of John: for the works which the Father hath given me to finish, the same works that I do." And on the last night before His death, in that wonderful high priestly prayer, we find Him saying, "I have glorified thee on the earth: I have finished the work which thou gavest me to do" (John 17:4).

The mission upon which God had sent His Son into the world was now accomplished. It was not actually finished till He breathed His last, but death was only an instant ahead, and in anticipation of it He cries "It is finished." The demanding work is done. The divinely-given task is performed. A work more honorable and momentous than ever entrusted to man or angels, has been completed. That for which He had left heaven's glory that for which He had taken upon Him the form of a servant, that for which He had remained upon earth for thirty-three years to do, was now consummated. Nothing remained to be added. The goal of the Incarnation is reached. With what joyous triumph must He here have viewed the costly work which, committed to Him, had now been perfected!

"It is finished." The mission upon which God had sent His Son into the world was accomplished. That which had been eternally purposed had come to pass. The plan of God had been fully carried out.

Because He is the Most High, God's will, cannot be thwarted. Because He is supreme, God's counsel must stand. Because He is almighty, God's purpose cannot be overthrown.

"But he is in one mind, and who can turn him? And what his soul desireth, even that he doeth" (Job 23:13). "I know that thou canst do everything, and that no thought can be withholding from thee" (Job 42:2). "But our God is in the heavens: He hath done whatsoever he hath pleased" (Psa 115:3). "There is no wisdom nor understanding nor counsel against the Lord" (Pro 21:30). "For the Lord of hosts hath purposed, and who shall disannul it? And His hand is stretched out, and who shall turn it back?" (Isa 14:27). "Remember the former things of old: for I am God, and there is none else; I am God, and there is none like me: Declaring the end from the beginning, and from ancient times the things that are not yet done, saying, My counsel shall stand, and I will do all my pleasure" (Isa 46:9-10). "And all the inhabitants of the earth are reputed as nothing: and he doeth according to his will in the army of heaven, and among the inhabitants of the earth: and none can stay his hand, or say unto him, What doest thou?" (Dan 4:35). And, in the triumphant cry of the Jesus— "It is finished"—we have a prophecy and pledge of the ultimate carrying out of God's plan completely. At the end of time, when everything is wound up, and God's purpose has been fully consummated, when everything has been done which He before determined should be done, then shall it be said again, "It is finished."

"It is finished."

4. Here we see the accomplishment of the Atonement. Above we have spoken of Christ reaching the goal of the Incarnation, and of the consummation of His mission to the earth; what that goal and mission was, the Scriptures plainly reveal. The Son of Man came here "to seek and to save that which was lost" (Luke 19:10). Christ Jesus came into the world "to save sinners" (1Ti 1:15). God sent forth His Son, born of a woman, "to redeem them that were under the law" (Gal 4:5). He was manifested "to take away our sins" (1Jo 3:5). And all this involved the Cross. The "lost" which He came to seek could only be found there—in the place of death and under the condemnation of God. Sinners could be "saved" only by One taking their place and bearing their iniquities. They who were under the Law could be "redeemed" only by Another fulfilling its requirements and suffering its curse. Our sins could be "taken away" only by their being blotted out by the precious blood of Christ. The demands of justice must be met; the requirements of God's holiness must be satisfied; the awful debt we incurred must be paid. And on the Cross, this was done; done by none less than the Son of God; done perfectly; done once for all.

"It is finished."

That to which so many types looked forward, was now accomplished. A covering from sin and its shame, typified by the coats of skin with which the Lord God clothed our first parents, was now provided. The more excellent sacrifice, typified by Abel's lamb, had now been offered. A shelter from the storm of divine judgment, typified by the Ark of Noah, was now furnished. The only-begotten and well-beloved Son, typified by Abraham's offering up of Isaac, had already been placed upon the altar. A protection from the avenging angel, typified by the shed blood of the Passover-lamb, was now supplied. A cure from the serpent's bite, typified by the serpent of brass upon the pole, was now made ready for sinners. The providing of a life-giving fountain, typified by Moses striking the rock, was now affected.

"It is finished." The Greek word here, teleo, is translated variously in the New Testament. A glance at some of the different renderings in other passages will enable us to discern the fullness and finality of the term used by Jesus. In Matthew 11:1, teleo is rendered as follows, "When Jesus had made an end of commanding his twelve disciples, he departed thence." In Matthew 17:24 it is rendered, "They that received tribute money came to Peter, and said, Doth not your master pay tribute?" In Luke 2:39, it is rendered, "And when they had performed all things according to the Law of the Lord, they returned into Galilee." In Luke 18:31, it is rendered, "All things that are written by the prophets concerning the Son shall be accomplished."

"It is finished." He cried: it is "made an end of"; it is "paid"; it is "performed"; it is "accomplished." What was made an end of? —our sins and their guilt. What was "paid?"—the price of our redemption. What was "performed?"—the utmost requirements of the Law. What was "accomplished?"—the work which the Father had given Him to do. What was "finished?"—the making of atonement. God has furnished at least four proofs that Christ did finish the work which was given Him to do. First, in the rending of the veil, which showed that the way to God was now open. Second, in the raising of Christ from the dead, which evidenced that God had accepted His sacrifice. Third, the exaltation of Christ to His own right hand, which demonstrated the value of Christ's work and the Father's delight in His person. Fourth, the sending to earth of the Holy Spirit to apply the virtues and benefits of Christ's atoning death.

"It is finished." What was "finished?"—the work of atonement. What is the value of that to us? This: to the sinner, it is a message of glad tidings. All that a Holy God requires has been done. Nothing is left for the sinner to add. No works from us are demanded as the price of our salvation. All that is necessary for the sinner is to rest now by faith upon what Christ did. "The gift of God is eternal life through Jesus Christ our Lord" (Rom 6:23). To the believer, the knowledge that the atoning work of Christ is finished brings a sweet relief over against all the defects and imperfections of his services. There is nothing "finished" that we do: all our duties are imperfect. There is much of sin and vanity in the very best of our efforts, but the grand relief is that we are "complete" in Christ (Col 2:10)! Christ and His finished work are the ground of all our hopes. "It is finished."

5. Here we see the end of our sins. The sins of the believer, all of them, were transferred to the Jesus. As the Scripture says, "The Lord hath laid on him the iniquities of us all" (Isa 53:6). If then God laid my iniquities on Christ, they are no longer on me. Sin there is in me, for the old Adamic nature remains in the believer till death or till Christ's return, should He come before I die; but there is no sin on me. This distinction between sin in and sin on, is a vital one, and there should be little difficulty in apprehending it. If I were to say the judge passed sentence on a criminal, and that he is now under sentence of death, everyone would understand what I meant. In like manner, everyone out of Christ has the sentence of God's condemnation resting upon him. But when a sinner believes in the Lord Jesus, and receives Him as his Lord and Master, obey the salvation message according to (Acts 2:38-39) he is no longer "under condemnation"— sin is no longer on him, that is, the guilt, the condemnation, the penalty of sin, is no longer upon

him. And why? Because Christ bore our sins in His own body on the tree (1Pe 2:24)—the guilt, condemnation, and penalty of our sins, was transferred to our substitute. Hence, because my sins were transferred to Christ, they are no more upon me.

This precious truth was strikingly illustrated in Old Testament times regarding Israel's annual Day of Atonement. On that day, Aaron, the high priest (a type of Christ), made satisfaction to God for the sins which Israel had committed during the previous year. The way this was done is described in Leviticus 16. Two goats were taken and presented before the Lord at the door of the tabernacle: this was before anything was done with them: it represented Christ being sent and presenting Himself, offering to come into this world and be the Savior of sinners. One of the goats was then taken and killed, and its blood was carried into the tabernacle, within the veil, into the Holy of Holies, and there it was sprinkled before and upon the mercy seat—foreshadowing Christ offering Himself as a sacrifice, to meet the demands of His justice and satisfy the requirements of His holiness.

Then we read that Aaron came out of the tabernacle and laid both his hands upon the head of the second (living) goat— signifying an act of identification by which Aaron is the representative of the whole nation, identified the people with it, acknowledging that its doom was what their sins merited, and which, today, corresponds with the hands of faith laying hold of Christ and identifying ourselves with Him in His Death. Having laid his hands on the head of the live goat, Aaron now confessed over him "all the iniquities of the children of Israel, and all their transgressions in all their sins, putting them upon the head of the goat" (Lev 16:21). Thus, were Israel's sins transferred to their substitute. Finally, we are told, "And the goat shall bear upon him all their iniquities unto a land not inhabited: and he shall let go the goat in the wilderness" (Lev 16:22). The goat bearing Israel's sins, was taken unto an uninhabited wilderness, and the people of God saw him and their sins no more! In type this was Christ taking our sins into that desolate land where God was not and there making an end of them. The Cross of Christ then is the grave of our sins!

"It is finished."
6. Here we see the fulfillment of the Law's requirements. "The law is holy, and the commandment holy, and just and good" (Rom 7:12). How could it be anything less when Jehovah Himself had framed and given it! The fault lay not in the Law but in man who, being depraved and sinful, could not keep it. Yet that Law must be kept, and kept by a man, so that the Law might be honored and magnified, and its giver vindicated. Therefore, we read, "For what the law could not do, in that it was weak through the flesh, God sending his own Son, in the likeness of sinful flesh, and for sin, condemned sin in the flesh: that the righteousness of the law might be fulfilled in [not by] us, who walk not after flesh, but after the Spirit" (Rom 8:3-4). The "weakness" here is that of fallen man. The sending forth of God's Son in the likeness of sin's flesh (Greek) refers to the Incarnation: as we read in another Scripture, "God sent forth his Son, born of a woman, born under the law, that he might redeem them that were under the law" (Gal 4:4-5 RV). Yes, the Jesus was born "under the law," born under it that He might keep it perfectly in thought, word, and deed. "Think not that I am come to destroy the law, or the prophets: I am not come to destroy, but to fulfill" (Mat 5:17); such was His claim.

But not only did Jesus keep the precepts of the Law, He also suffered its penalty and endured its curse. We had broken it, and taking our place, He must receive its just sentence. Having received its penalty and endured its curse, the demands of the Law are fully met, and justice is satisfied. Therefore, is it written of believers, "Christ hath redeemed us from the curse of the law, being made a curse for us" (Gal 3:13). And again, "For Christ is the end of the law for righteousness to everyone that believeth" (Rom 10:4). And yet again, "For ye are not under the law, but under grace" (Rom 6:14). "It is finished." "Free from the Law, Jesus hath bled, and there is remission, cursed by the law and bruised by the fall, Grace hath redeemed us once for all."

7. Here we see the destruction of Satan's power. See it by faith. The Cross sounded the death of the devil's power. To human appearances it looked like the moment of his greatest triumph, yet, it was the hour of his ultimate defeat. In view of the Cross Jesus declared, "Now is the judgment of this world: now shall the prince of this world be cast out" (Joh 12:31). It is true that Satan has not yet been chained and cast into the bottomless pit, nevertheless, sentence has been passed (though not yet executed); his doom is certain; and his power is already broken so far as believers are concerned.

For the Christian, the devil is a vanquished foe. He was defeated by Christ at the Cross— "that through death he might destroy him that had the power of death, that is, the devil" (Hebrew 2:14). Believers have already been "delivered from the power of darkness" and translated into the kingdom of God's dear Son (Col 1:13). Satan, then, should be treated as a defeated enemy. No longer has he any legitimate claim upon us. Once we were his lawful "captives"; but now God worketh in us both to will and to do of His good pleasure. All that we now must do is to "resist the devil," and the promise is, "he will flee from you" (James 4:7).

"It is finished." Here was the triumphant answer to the rage of man and the enmity of Satan. It tells of the perfect work which meets sin in the place of judgment. All was completed just as God would have it, just as the prophets had foretold, just as the Old Testament ceremonial had foreshadowed, just as divine holiness demanded, and just as sinners needed. How strikingly appropriate is this sixth Cross-utterance of Jesus found in John's Gospel—the Gospel which displays the glory of Christ's deity! He seals it with His own words, attesting it is complete, and giving it the all-sufficient sanction of His own approval. Jesus says, "It is finished"—who then dare doubt or question it.

"It is finished." Reader, do you believe it? or, are you trying to add something of your own to the finished work of Christ to secure the favor of God? All you must do is to accept the pardon which He purchased. God is satisfied with His work on the cross, why are not you? Sinner, the moment you believe Jesus' testimony that it is finished, that moment every sin you have committed is blotted out, and you stand accepted in Christ! O would you not like to possess the assurance that there is nothing between your soul and God? Would you not like to know that every sin had been atoned for and put away? Then believe what God's Word says about Christ's death. Rest not on your feelings and experiences but on the written Word. There is only one way of finding peace, deliverance, wholeness, salvation, victory over the "it" and that is through faith in the shed blood of Jesus the of Lamb God. It is time to "Get Rid of "it", Before "it" Gets Rid of You".

"It is finished." Do you really believe it? Or, are you endeavoring to add something of your own to it and thus merit the favor of God? By continuing to hold on and struggle, seeking other sources to deal with the "it" in your life, you are nullifying the finished work of Christ by your own miserable additions to it!". The Gospel of God's grace, and the finished work of Christ is sufficient for our souls to rest upon. In the pages of this book, God uses forceful object lessons and His Word to show you, "How to Get Rid of "it", before "it" Gets Rid of You". It is a grave mistake not to embrace the Word of God, and cast yourself by faith upon what Christ had done for you.

Victory was given to us by way of the cross. Whatever your "it" or "its" might be, "it" has come to kill, steal and destroy you. Make a conscious effort to explore this information given in this book and expose the enemy of your soul. Let's "Get Rid of "it". After all, "It is Finished"

CHAPTER ONE

What is "it"?

We are all created with a basic need to be loved. God created us to both give and receive love, but though damaged emotions, our capacity to receive love can be dramatically hindered. Ignorance of God's love will also hinder us from receiving the great and glorious love that He has for us. **The root of most "its" is a lack of love being received by that person.** Many of us have been damaged emotionally by rejection, abandonment, abuse, etc., and thereby our capacity to receive love has been reduced. **Only an emotionally healthy person is capable of both giving and receiving love as God intended.**

Self-worth issues can hinder love

Self-worth issues are rooted in believing that we are not worthy or deserve to be loved. When we believe that we are unlovable, we will unconsciously reject any love that comes our way. We won't believe the love, because we believe in our hearts that we are not worthy. **Self-worth issues are all rooted in our failing to see who we really are in Christ.**

If you walked into a gallery of world-class art, and pointed to a painting, saying, "That is the ugliest thing I've ever seen! Who painted that??" Now let's say the artist was standing right next to you. How do you think that would make him feel? Do you realize we are the artwork of God, a special painting crafted together by the master painter? Do you think it brings Him honor when we look down on ourselves? **We need to stop putting down what God has made.**

Many times, we have self-unforgiveness issues because we blame ourselves for something, or we've done something we deeply regret, and we simply cannot let it go. We need to realize that Jesus has forgiven us of all our failures, and we need to start seeing ourselves as forgiven. Otherwise, we're denying the work of Christ in our life! **If God forgave you, and you're still beating yourself up, then you don't really believe what Jesus did for you.** It's that simple!

Just as we must forgive others (see Matthew 18:21-35), we need to forgive ourselves just the same. Self-hate has been known to be the root behind diseases such as lupus and Crohn's disease, as well as other auto-immune diseases. We need to stop holding ourselves accountable for that which Jesus has set us free from.

If we want to be in faith, we need to BELIEVE what Jesus did for us, and part of that believing is seeing ourselves as forgiven and clothed with the righteousness of God, which is upon all who believe in the finished work of Christ. Without faith, it is impossible to please God (see Hebrews 11:6), so if you want to please God, start taking the finished work of the cross seriously, and begin to see yourself as forgiven, washed clean, and clothed in the righteousness of God. For the righteousness (right standing with God) is upon all who believe:

"Even the righteousness of God which is by faith of Jesus Christ unto all and upon all them that believe..." (Romans 3:22 KJV)

Unforgiveness is rooted in a lack of realization of how much God has forgiven us, and therefore we're not thankful for the steep and terrible price that Jesus paid for our own failures. Therefore, it is so important to mediate on what Jesus did for us, until it transforms our heart. The message of Jesus' work for us is what causes faith to arise in our hearts and transforms us from the inside out (read Romans 10:8-17).

Learning to see yourself as God sees you, and forgive yourself because you want to please God and be in faith and be thankful for what Jesus did for you, is the biggest step in overcoming self-worth issues. Of course, there are spirits that may need to be driven out as well, such as self-hate, guilt, condemnation, etc.

Receiving the love God has for us

When it comes to God's love for us, that's obvious, considering how He loves even the sinner so much that Jesus came to die for them. Anybody who knows the message of the cross, has some knowledge of God's love for us. However, many times, we blame God for our problems, and so we don't believe the love that He has for us. Not only do we blame Him for our problems, many times we think that God gave us the sickness or problem in our life to teach us something. Nothing could be further from the truth! Jesus tells us clearly who came to kill, steal, and destroy, and who came so that we could have life and have it in abundance.

"The thief cometh not, but for to steal, and to kill, and to destroy: I am come that they might have life, and that they might have it more abundantly." (John 10:10 KJV)

If we are going to receive the love that God has for us, we need to get our thinking straightened out. He's not the one behind our problems, but rather Jesus paid the full price so that we can be forgiven all our sins, both physically and emotionally healed, and blessed.

"When the even was come, they brought unto him many that were possessed with devils: and he cast out the spirits with his word, and healed all that were

Look at how good God's heart is toward mankind! Not only did Jesus heal them, but He proved the blessings of the covenant we have with Him today concerning our healing and deliverance. Isn't He good toward us? **The reason why things happen to us, is because we live in a fallen world that is under the control of the evil one.** It's not God's fault. He loves you. Jesus died for you.

Settling the fact that God loves you and is good toward you is crucial to restoring your God-given capacity to receive His love. If you can't receive His love, then you need to stop and ask yourself four questions:

1. Am I blaming God for anything bad that happened to me?

2. Have I been emotionally wounded in such a way that it is hindering my ability to freely receive love as God intended me to?

3. Do I have knowledge and revelation of how much God loves me? Do I have a solid Biblical understanding of how I am loved with the same kind of love that the Father has for Jesus?

4. Is there a self-worth issue that makes me feel unworthy to be loved?

Settling these issues lays a foundation for breaking free from the power of the "IT". You must repair the damage and faulty thinking which hinders your ability to receive the love that God has for you.

How do you know if you are receiving God's love or if it's hindered? **If you are not passionate about Jesus, then somewhere your ability to receive His love is hindered.**

If you are living a life without receiving God's love in your heart daily, you are missing out on the most fulfilling life you can have here on this earth. To know God's love, which surpasses all understanding (see Philippians 4:7), dispels all our fears and gives us a sense of peace and joy that we could never otherwise know.

What exactly is "it'?

An "it" is formed when we try to use something other than God, to meet our need to be loved. When our ability to receive God's love into our hearts is hindered, we will feel like something is missing, and seek to fill that void with something else. When that thing, whatever it might be, fills that void, we grow to love "it" because it's meeting a need. Over time, we establish a relationship with that thing, and when it comes time to depart, it's like breaking up a relationship. That's why the "it" is so destructive; we've relied on that thing to meet a need and we've established a relationship with it. Now when it's time to break up the love, it isn't so easy to say goodbye.

One widespread problem that we see when we try to deal with "it", is where we give up one "it" successfully, only to find yourself with another "it". We might quit drinking only to start overeating, for example. We might think we're finding victory, but all we're really doing is trading one "it" for another "it". This is because something must fill the love-void in our hearts, and if it's not one thing, it will be another.

What about cutting or self-harm?

Cutting or self-mutation is a special type of "it", where there's a need to either release pain in a person's heart or the person believes that they deserve to be punished for their failures. In these cases, the person certainly has an issue receiving the love that God has for them but there's another type of root that needs to be addressed as well. There's emotional pain or guilt that the person is dealing with that needs to be resolved. Finding out what happened and receiving Christ's truth concerning those areas is important for their healing. Any bondage involving guilt will need to be resolved through realizing and accepting the work of Christ on the cross for that person and they will likely need spirits of guilt, condemnation, self-hate, etc. driven out in Jesus' name. Again, getting the person to see them self for who they really are in Christ, forgiven, loved, and blessed, is crucial to lasting freedom from self-hate issues.

See yourself as lovable!

The key in uprooting most "its" is to deal with the underlying issues which are limiting their capacity to freely receive love from God and others, along with dealing with any self-worth issues by establishing an understanding of your true identity in Christ. **Coming to a place where you believe you are lovable is key to receiving love in general,** so dealing with self-worth issues is an important key to breaking down the walls which keep us from feeling loved. The only way to obtain a true sense of worth and value is to get a revelation of how much you are loved by God, who sent His son Jesus to die for you.

Discovering the root

To discover the root of your "it", you need to get real honest with yourself. Many times, we are in denial about the pain we are feeling. Figuring out what is the root of a bondage is all about asking the right questions, and that is especially important when it comes to uprooting an "it". Why don't we feel loved? Do we feel unlovable? (Let's stop right there; if we feel unlovable, then you've just discovered a self-worth issue that will need to be addressed.) Are you passionate about Jesus? If not, then something in hindering you from realizing how much you are loved by Him who died for you. Do you see yourself as forgiven and loved by the God because of what He did for you?

As you discover emotional wounds, you'll need to forgive (others, yourself, and God) and invite Jesus to come and heal the damage in your heart. If you don't realize how much God loves you, then you'll need to spend some time learning about what Jesus did for you on the cross, and what a terrible price He paid because He loved you so very much. Often breaking out of an "it" is a combination of emotional healing, learning about who you are in Christ, forgiving (yourself, others, and God), overcoming self-worth issues by changing how you see yourself (in light of how God sees and loves you), and casting out any spirits that came in and are enforcing the destructive behavior. Spirits behind guilt, condemnation, etc. also need to be driven out, as they seek to keep us from fully seeing what Jesus did for us on the cross.

Dealing with the issues underlying an "it" is key to uprooting it permanently. If you want lasting freedom and wholeness in this area of your life, you will have to deal with the issues that have limited your capacity to receive love, especially the love that God has for you.

CHAPTER TWO

The "it" of Trials, Troubles, and Adversities

DEFINITION: A trial is an examination by testing. Biblically, it is a test of faith in which you experience trouble or adversity. Trouble is sometimes referred to as "tribulation" in the Bible. Adversity is similar to trouble, meaning extremely unfavorable experiences.

FACTS ABOUT TRIALS, TROUBLES, AND ADVERSITIES:

A trial is not a temptation. A temptation is something that entices you to sin (see the topic of "Temptation" in this database). A trial is an adversity you are experiencing that tests your faith.

Trials, troubles, and adversities are experienced by all believers. In fact, the apostles taught believers that they would only enter the Kingdom of God through adversity (Acts 14:22). Peter said not to consider it strange or unusual when you encounter trouble (1 Peter 4:12).

God uses both positive and negative experiences for your good. Joseph told his brothers: *"You intended to harm me, but God intended it for good to accomplish what is now being done, the saving of many lives" (Genesis 50:20).* The Apostle Paul declared: *"And we know that in all things God works for the good of those who love him, who have been called according to his purpose" (Romans 8:28)*

DEALING WITH TRIALS, TROUBLES, AND ADVERSITIES:

Expect to experience adversity. Peter said not to be surprised by it (1 Peter 4:12-16). The apostles taught the early church that it was to be experienced as part of living in the Kingdom of God (Acts 14:22).

Pray about your trials, troubles and adversities. The Bible says that God has promised to hear before you call and even while you are yet speaking (Isaiah 65:24). Confess your total dependence on Him. Instead of asking "What am I going to do in this adversity?" ask God, "What are You going to do?"

Immerse yourself in the Word of God. The Bible brings comfort and direction during trials, troubles, and adversities.

Use your spiritual weapons. Trials, troubles, and adverse circumstances must be faced with your spiritual weapons. Study Ephesians 6:10-18. See also "Spiritual Warfare" in this database.

Remember that good things come from God. If something comes to rob, steal, or destroy in your life, do not blame God. It is from the enemy. Jesus said: *"The thief comes only to steal and kill and destroy; I have come that they may have life, and have it to the full" (John 10:10).* James said: *"Don't be deceived, my dear brothers. Every good and perfect gift is from above,* *coming down from the Father of the heavenly lights, who does not change like shifting shadows"* (James 1:16-17).

Remember that there is divine purpose in adversity. Your faith is being refined (1 Peter 1:6-7) and spiritual qualities are being developed in your life: *"Not only so, but we also rejoice in our sufferings, because we know that suffering produces perseverance; perseverance, character; and character, hope" (Romans 5:3-4).*

Focus on eternal benefits. The Bible indicates that trials actually work for you when you are focused on the eternal benefits of the trials instead of the temporary problems: *"Therefore we do not lose heart. Even though our outward man is perishing, yet the inward man is being renewed day by day. For our light affliction, which is but for a moment, is working for us a far more exceeding and eternal weight of glory, while we do not look at the things which are seen, but at the things which are not seen. For the things which are seen are temporary, but the things which are not seen are eternal" (2 Corinthians 4:16-18).*

Rejoice in times of adversity. The Bible commands you to rejoice and give thanks to God in times of adversity.   You may not feel like doing this, but do it as an act of your will   (See 1 Thessalonians 5:18 and 1 Peter 1:6-7; 4:12-17). You do not give thanks for the adversity, but in the midst of and in spite of it.

Remember these six "p"s of adversity.
      -Purpose: God has divine purpose in your trial.
      -Profitable: Your trial is profitable if you submit to God and trust Him.
      -Presence: God will be with you in your trials.
      -Prove: Your faith will be proven by the difficulties.
      -Produce: Your trial will produce positive spiritual qualities in your life.
      -Perspective: You will emerge with a new perspective.

WHAT GOD'S WORD SAYS ABOUT TRIALS, TROUBLES, AND ADVERSITIES:

You intended to harm me, but God intended it for good to accomplish what is now being done, the saving of many lives. (Genesis 50:20)

But in their distress, they turned to the Lord, the God of Israel, and sought him, and he was found by them. (2 Chronicles 15:4)

Have I not commanded you? Be strong and courageous. Do not be terrified; do not be discouraged, for the Lord your God will be with you wherever you go. (Joshua 1:9)

The Lord is a refuge for the oppressed, a stronghold in times of trouble. (Psalm 9:9)

Do not be far from me, for trouble is near and there is no one to help. (Psalm 22:11)

The troubles of my heart have multiplied; free me from my anguish. (Psalm 25:17)

For in the day of trouble he will keep me safe in his dwelling; he will hide me in the shelter of his tabernacle and set me high upon a rock. (Psalm 27:5)

I will be glad and rejoice in your love, for you saw my affliction and knew the anguish of my soul. You have not handed me over to the enemy but have set my feet in a spacious place. (Psalm 31:8)

You are my hiding place; you will protect me from trouble and surround me with songs of deliverance. (Psalm 32:7)

This poor man called, and the Lord heard him; he saved him out of all his troubles. The angel of the Lord encamps around those who fear him, and he delivers them. (Psalm 34:6)

The righteous cry out, and the Lord hears them; he delivers them from all their troubles. The Lord is close to the brokenhearted and saves those who are crushed in spirit. A righteous man may have many troubles, but the Lord delivers him from them all. (Psalm 34:17-19)

May all who gloat over my distress be put to shame and confusion. (Psalm 35:26)

The salvation of the righteous comes from the Lord; he is their stronghold in time of trouble. The Lord helps them and delivers them; he delivers them from the wicked and saves them, because they take refuge in him. (Psalm 37:39-40)

For troubles without number surround me; my sins have overtaken me, and I cannot see. They are more than the hairs of my head, and my heart fails within me. (Psalm 40:12)

God is our refuge and strength, an ever-present help in trouble. (Psalm 46:1)

...call upon me in the day of trouble; I will deliver you, and you will honor me. (Psalm 50:15)

But I will sing of your strength, in the morning I will sing of your love; for you are my fortress, my refuge in times of trouble. (Psalms 59:16)

Do not hide your face from your servant; answer me quickly, for I am in trouble. (Psalm 69:17)

In the day of my trouble I will call to you, for you will answer me. (Psalm 86:7)

He will call upon me, and I will answer him; I will be with him in trouble, I will deliver him and honor him. (Psalms 91:15)

Do not hide your face from me when I am in distress. Turn your ear to me; when I call, answer me quickly. (Psalms 102:2)

Give us aid against the enemy, for the help of man is worthless. With God we will gain the victory, and he will trample down our enemies. (Psalms 108:12-13)

Trouble and distress have come upon me, but your commands are my delight. (Psalm 119:143)

Though I walk in the midst of trouble, you preserve my life; you stretch out your hand against the anger of my foes, with your right hand you save me. The Lord will fulfill [his purpose] for me; your love, O Lord, endures forever--do not abandon the works of your hands. (Psalms 138:7-8)

I pour out my complaint before him; before him I tell my trouble. (Psalm 142:2)

For your name's sake, O Lord, preserve my life; in your righteousness, bring me out of trouble. (Psalms 143:11)

If you falter in times of trouble, how small is your strength! (Proverbs 24:10)

For I am the Lord, your God, who takes hold of your right hand and says to you, Do not fear; I will help you. (Isaiah 41:13)

Shout for joy, O heavens; rejoice, O earth; burst into song, O mountains! For the Lord comforts his people and will have compassion on his afflicted ones. (Isaiah 49:13)

... no weapon forged against you will prevail, and you will refute every tongue that accuses you. (Isaiah 54:17)

Before they call I will answer; while they are still speaking I will hear. (Isaiah 65:24)

The Lord is good, A stronghold in the day of trouble; And He knows those who trust in Him. (Nahum 1:7)

The thief comes only to steal and kill and destroy; I have come that they may have life, and have it to the full. (John 10:10)

Do not let your hearts be troubled and do not be afraid. (John 14:27)

In this world you will have trouble. But take heart! I have overcome the world. (John 16:33)

They preached the good news in that city and won a large number of disciples. Then they returned to Lystra, Iconium and Antioch, strengthening the disciples and encouraging them to remain true to the faith. "We must go through many hardships to enter the kingdom of God," they said. (Acts 14:22)

Not only so, but we also rejoice in our sufferings, because we know that suffering produces perseverance; perseverance, character; and character, hope. (Romans 5:3-4).

And we know that in all things God works for the good of those who love him, who have been called according to his purpose. (Romans 8:28)

Who shall separate us from the love of Christ? Shall trouble or hardship or persecution or famine or nakedness or danger or sword? As it is written: "For your sake we face death all day long; we are considered as sheep to be slaughtered."   No, in all these things we are more than conquerors through him who loved us. For I am convinced that neither death nor life, neither angels nor demons, neither the present nor the future, nor any powers, neither height nor depth, nor anything else in all creation, will be able to separate us from the love of God that is in Christ Jesus our Lord. (Romans 8:35-39)

Be joyful in hope, patient in affliction, faithful in prayer. (Romans 12:12)

Praise be to the God and Father of our Lord Jesus Christ, the Father of compassion and the God of all comfort, who comforts us in all our troubles, so that we can comfort those in any trouble with the comfort we ourselves have received from God. For just as the sufferings of Christ flow over into our lives, so also through Christ our comfort overflows. (2 Corinthians 1:3-5)

Therefore, we do not lose heart. Even though our outward man is perishing, yet the inward man is being renewed day by day. For our light affliction, which is but for a moment, is working for us a far more exceeding and eternal weight of glory, while we do not look at the things which are seen, but at the things which are not seen. For the things which are seen are temporary, but the things which are not seen are eternal. (2 Corinthians 4:16-18)

But he said to me, "My grace is sufficient for you, for my power is made perfect in weakness." Therefore, I will boast all the more gladly about my weaknesses, so that Christ's power may rest on me. That is why, for Christ's sake, I delight in weaknesses, in insults, in hardships, in persecutions, in difficulties. For when I am weak, then I am strong. (2 Corinthians 12:9)

Do not be anxious about anything, but in everything, by prayer and petition, with thanksgiving, present your requests to God. And the peace of God, which transcends all understanding, will guard your hearts and your minds in Christ Jesus. (Philippians 4:6-7)

... that no one should be shaken by these afflictions; for you yourselves know that we are appointed to this. (1 Thessalonians 3:3, NKJV)

Give thanks in all circumstances, for this is God's will for you in Christ Jesus. (1 Thessalonians 5:18)

Blessed is the man who perseveres under trial, because when he has stood the test, he will receive the crown of life that God has promised to those who love him. (James 1:12)

Don't be deceived, my dear brothers. Every good and perfect gift is from above, coming down from the Father of the heavenly lights, who does not change like shifting shadows. (James 1:16-17).

Is any one of you in trouble? He should pray. (James 5:13)

In this you greatly rejoice, though now for a little while you may have had to suffer grief in all kinds of trials. These have come so that your faith--of greater worth than gold, which perishes even though refined by fire--may be proved genuine and may result in praise, glory and honor when Jesus Christ is revealed. (1 Peter 1:6-7)

Dear friends, do not be surprised at the painful trial you are suffering, as though something strange were happening to you. But rejoice that you participate in the sufferings of Christ, so that you may be overjoyed when his glory is revealed. If you are insulted because of the name of Christ, you are blessed, for the Spirit of glory and of God rests on you. If you suffer, it should not be as a murderer or thief or any other kind of criminal, or even as a meddler. However, if you suffer as a Christian, do not be ashamed, but praise God that you bear that name. (1 Peter 4:12-17)

Cast all your anxiety on him because he cares for you. Be self-controlled and alert. Your enemy the devil prowls around like a roaring lion looking for someone to devour. Resist him, standing firm in the faith, because you know that your brothers throughout the world are undergoing the same kind of sufferings. And the God of all grace, who called you to his eternal glory in Christ, after you have suffered a little while, will himself restore you and make you strong, firm and steadfast. (1 Peter 5:7-10)

Study the story of Job--especially chapters 1-2 and chapter 42--to understand more about the purpose of trials.

CHAPTER THREE

The "it" of Dissatisfaction
(Unhappiness)

DEFINITION: Dissatisfaction is a feeling of discontent and displeasure with circumstances in life or other people. It is a feeling of unhappiness.

FACTS ABOUT DISSATISFACTION:

The enemy causes dissatisfaction. The Bible says in John 10:10 that it is the enemy that kills, steals, and destroys. If you are dissatisfied and unhappy, guess who stole your joy? Jesus came to destroy the work of the enemy and to give you abundant life. He wants you to be content and happy.

Disappointments cause dissatisfaction. Sometimes people disappoint you or your circumstances are disappointing. Sometimes you disappoint yourself by failures. Such disappointments can lead to dissatisfaction. Dissatisfaction with your own performance or that of others leads to discouragement, and discouragement can lead to depression.

Materialism causes dissatisfaction. The Apostle Paul warned Timothy: *"People who want to get rich fall into temptation and a trap and into many foolish and harmful desires that plunge men into ruin and destruction. For the love of money is a root of all kinds of evil. Some people, eager for money, have wandered from the faith and pierced themselves with many griefs" (1 Timothy 6:9-10).* All the things that you want that seem so important are usually temporal. Focus on the eternal (1 John 2:15-17).

Dissatisfaction is sin. When you are dissatisfied, grumbling, and complaining, you are actually blaming God for your circumstances, implying that He is not providing adequately for your wants and needs. Israel was repeatedly dissatisfied with God's provision in the wilderness. They grumbled about lack of water and food. Then they complained because the manna God provided was not as good as the leeks and garlic they had in Egypt. God said their grumbling was sin, and judged it as such.

Dissatisfaction leads to grumbling, complaining, unhappiness, and an unthankful and critical spirit.

DEALING WITH DISSATISFACTION:

Recognize that dissatisfaction is sin. As with other sins, you must confess and ask God for forgiveness.

Ask God to give you a spirit of contentment. The Apostle Paul declared: *"...I have learned to be content whatever the circumstances. I know what it is to be in need, and I know what it is to have plenty. I have learned the secret of being content in any and every situation, whether well fed or hungry, whether living in plenty or in want. I can do everything through him who gives me*

27

strength" (Philippians 4:11-13). He told young Timothy to be content with the basics of food and clothing (1 Timothy 6:8). The Hebrews were admonished to be content with what they had. **Put your trust in God**, rather than in people or things that will fail (Psalm 20:7-8; 44:6; 146:3). That way you will never be disappointed or dissatisfied. Your trust should be in God, not in man. Keep your focus on the Lord!

Make positive changes in your life. What changes can you make that will eliminate negative circumstances in your life? What changes will bring joy back into your life?

Return to the basics of Christian life. Be faithful in prayer, church attendance, and the Word of God. The Word of God is effective to facilitate change in any problem or circumstance of your life. Dissatisfaction is a state of mind, and your mind can be renewed through the Word (Ephesians 4:23; Colossians 3:10).

Cultivate friendships with positive people. Avoid being a loner. Satan wants to isolate you through dissatisfaction. Deliberately spend time with believers who are positive and uplifting. Do not hang out with negative, critical, judgmental people, as this will contribute to your own dissatisfaction. Christian friendships with positive people will help you when you feel discouraged (Ecclesiastes 4:9-10).

Do something for others. This will take the focus off of things that are causing your dissatisfaction. The joy you receive from doing acts of kindness will help eliminate your dissatisfaction. When you see how tough some other people have it, you will be more satisfied with your own lot in life.

Start a gratitude journal. Write down at least one thing each day for which you are thankful. This will help you remain focused on the positive instead of the negative. It is the will of God for you to give thanks in everything (1 Thessalonians 5:18).

Recognize the difference between happiness and joy. Happiness is based on outward circumstances. When things are going well, then you are happy. When circumstances are bad, you are unhappy. Joy, on the other hand, is a spiritual fruit from God. You can rejoice in every circumstance and the joy of the Lord gives you strength to face negative circumstances (Philippians 4:4, 1 Thessalonians 5:18). Jesus faced the most difficult circumstances of His life with joy. Although He knew the suffering that awaited Him in Jerusalem, He entered the city with a joyous procession. In view of this, *"Let us fix our eyes on Jesus, the author and perfecter of our faith, who for the joy set before him endured the cross"* (Hebrews 12:2).

Pray this prayer: *"Restore to me the joy of your salvation and grant me a willing spirit, to sustain me"* (Psalm 51:12).

WHAT GOD'S WORD SAYS ABOUT DISSATISFACTION:

...for the joy of the Lord is your strength. (Nehemiah 8:10)

Trust in the Lord and do good; dwell in the land and enjoy safe pasture. Delight yourself in the Lord and he will give you the desires of your heart.   (Psalms 37:3-4)

My soul thirsts for God, for the living God. When can I go and meet with God? (Psalm 42:2)

O God, you are my God, earnestly I seek you; my soul thirsts for you, my body longs for you, in a dry and weary land where there is no water. (Psalm 63:1)

My soul will be satisfied as with the richest of foods; with singing lips my mouth will praise you. (Psalm 63:5)

Satisfy us in the morning with your unfailing love, that we may sing for joy and be glad all our days. (Psalm 90:14)

With long life will I satisfy him and show him my salvation. (Psalm 91:16)

Praise the Lord, O my soul; all my inmost being, praise his holy name. Praise the Lord, O my soul, and forget not all his benefits--who forgives all your sins and heals all your diseases, who redeems your life from the pit and crowns you with love and compassion, who satisfies your desires with good things so that your youth is renewed like the eagle's. (Psalm 103:1-5)

For he satisfies the thirsty and fills the hungry with good things. (Psalm 107:9)

You open your hand and satisfy the desire of every living thing. (Psalm 145:16)

Do not put your trust in princes, in mortal men, who cannot save. (Psalms 146:3)

Why spend money on what is not bread, and your labor on what does not satisfy?
Listen, listen to me, and eat what is good and your soul will delight in the richest of fare.
Give ear and come to me; hear me, that your soul may live. (Isaiah 55:2-3)

The Lord will guide you always; he will satisfy your needs in a sun-scorched land and will strengthen your frame. You will be like a well-watered garden, like a spring whose waters never fail. (Isaiah 58:11)

Blessed are you who hunger now for you will be satisfied. (Luke 6:21)

Jesus answered, "Everyone who drinks this water will be thirsty again, but whoever drinks the water I give him will never thirst. Indeed, the water I give him will become in him a spring of water welling up to eternal life." (John 4:13-14)

For the bread of God is he who comes down from heaven and gives life to the world. (John 6:33)

I am the bread of life. He who comes to me will never go hungry, and he who believes in me will never be thirsty. (John 6:35)

If anyone is thirsty, let him come to me and drink. Whoever believes in me, as the Scripture has said, streams of living water will flow from within him. (John 7:38)

The thief comes only to steal and kill and destroy; I have come that they may have life, and have it to the full. (John 10:10)

I have told you this so that my joy may be in you and that your joy may be complete.
(John 15:11)

For the kingdom of God is not a matter of eating and drinking, but of righteousness, peace and joy in the Holy Spirit, (Romans 14:17)

But the fruit of the Spirit is love, joy, peace, patience, kindness, goodness, faithfulness, 23 gentleness and self-control. Against such things there is no law.   (Galatians 5:22-23)

Rejoice in the Lord always. I will say it again: Rejoice! Let your gentleness be evident to all. The Lord is near. Do not be anxious about anything, but in everything, by prayer and petition, with thanksgiving, present your requests to God. And the peace of God, which transcends all understanding, will guard your hearts and your minds in Christ Jesus. Finally, brothers, whatever is true, whatever is noble, whatever is right, whatever is pure, whatever is lovely, whatever is admirable--if anything is excellent or praiseworthy--think about such things. Whatever you have learned or received or heard from me, or seen in me--put it into practice. And the God of peace will be with you. (Philippians 4:4-9)

Not that I speak in respect of want: for I have learned, in whatsoever state I am, therewith to be content. I know both how to be abased, and I know how to abound: everywhere and in all things, I am instructed both to be full and to be hungry, both to abound and to suffer need. I can do all things through Christ which strengthened me. (Philippians 4:11-13)

And my God will meet all your needs according to his glorious riches in Christ Jesus.
(Philippians 4:19)

Be joyful always; pray continually; give thanks in all circumstances, for this is God's will for you in Christ Jesus. (1 Thessalonians 5:16-18)

But if we have food and clothing, we will be content with that. (1 Timothy 6:8)

People who want to get rich fall into temptation and a trap and into many foolish and harmful desires that plunge men into ruin and destruction. For the love of money is a root of all kinds of evil. Some people, eager for money, have wandered from the faith and pierced themselves with many griefs. (1 Timothy 6:9-10)

Keep your lives free from the love of money and be content with what you have, because God has said, "Never will I leave you; never will I forsake you."   (Hebrews 13:5)

Though you have not seen him, you love him; and even though you do not see him now, you believe in him and are filled with an inexpressible and glorious joy, for you are receiving the goal of your faith, the salvation of your souls. (1 Peter 1:8-9)

His divine power has given us everything we need for life and godliness through our knowledge of him who called us by his own glory and goodness. (2 Peter 1:3)

Do not love the world or anything in the world. If anyone loves the world, the love of the Father is not in him. For everything in the world--the cravings of sinful man, the lust of his eyes and the boasting of what he has and does--comes not from the Father but from the world. The world and its desires pass away, but the man who does the will of God lives forever. (1 John 2:15-17)

He will lead them to springs of living water. And God will wipe away every tear from their eyes. (Revelation 7:17)

"Come!" Whoever is thirsty, let him come; and whoever wishes, let him take the free gift of the water of life. (Revelation 22:17)

Read through the book of Psalms and underline all of the commands to rejoice and the reasons for rejoicing instead of being dissatisfied.

CHAPTER FOUR

The "it" of Pride

DEFINITION: Pride is a feeling of haughty superiority demonstrated by someone who thinks they are better than others. It is an inflated sense of one's self-worth, skills, intelligence, accomplishments, or position. Conceit, vanity, arrogance, boasting, egotism, and haughtiness are other words that describe pride.

FACTS ABOUT PRIDE:

Pride was the original sin. It was because of pride that Satan fell from his exalted position in heaven (Isaiah 14:13). It was the appeal of pride--knowing all things--that resulted in the first sin by mankind (Genesis 3).

Attributes of pride. Boasting is one evidence of pride. Another is putting other people down to elevate self and gloating over the misfortunes of others.   Pride is also marked by a haughty attitude and a tendency to perform good deeds in order to receive honor from men (Matthew 23:5-6, 13-16). Pride makes one self-sufficient apart from God. Pride deceives you into thinking you are better than others and that you cannot fall into sin. Pride keeps you from seeking God (Psalm 10:4) and exalts self against the knowledge of God (2 Corinthians 10:5).

Pride is a sin. Pride is rebellion against God because it attributes to self the honor due to God alone. God hates pride (Proverbs 6:16) and everyone who is proud is an abomination to the Lord (Proverbs 16:5).

Pride is the root of all sin. As the first sin, pride is the root of all sin. All sins can be traced back to the original root of pride.

DEALING WITH PRIDE:

Ask God to reveal pride in your life. Prideful behavior may have been such a part of your life that you do not even recognize its manifestations. Ask God to show you attitudes or attributes of pride in your life so you can deal with them.

Ask God for forgiveness. Pride is sin--in fact it is one of the seven sins most hated by God. As with any other sin, pride requires confession and repentance.

Humble yourself before God. Humility is the opposite of pride. We are commanded to "humble ourselves" as an act of our will (James 4:10). Seek to serve others rather than being a "star".

WHAT GOD'S WORD SAYS ABOUT PRIDE:

You will save the humble people; But Your eyes are on the haughty, that You may bring them down. (2 Samuel 22:28, NKJV)

Read 2 Kings 5: Naaman's pride almost caused him to miss a miracle!

In his arrogance the wicked man hunts down the weak, who are caught in the schemes he devises. He boasts of the cravings of his heart; he blesses the greedy and reviles the Lord. In his pride the wicked does not seek him; in all his thoughts there is no room for God. (Psalm 10:2-4)

May the Lord cut off all flattering lips and every boastful tongue that says, "We will triumph with our tongues; we own our lips--who is our master?" (Psalm 12:3)

You save the humble but bring low those whose eyes are haughty. (Psalm 18:27)

For in his own eyes he flatters himself too much to detect or hate his sin. (Psalm 36:2)

Blessed is the man who makes the Lord his trust, who does not look to the proud, to those who turn aside to false gods. (Psalm 40:4)

Why do you boast of evil, you mighty man? Why do you boast all day long, you who are a disgrace in the eyes of the God? (Psalm 52:1)

Therefore, pride is their necklace; they clothe themselves with violence. (Psalm 73:6)

Whoever has haughty eyes and a proud heart, him will I not endure. (Psalm 101:5)

Though the Lord is on high, he looks upon the lowly, but the proud he knows from afar. (Psalm 138:6)

He mocks proud mockers but gives grace to the humble. (Proverbs 3:34)

There are six things the Lord hates, seven that are detestable to him: haughty eyes, a lying tongue, hands that shed innocent blood, a heart that devises wicked schemes, feet that are quick to rush into evil, a false witness who pours out lies and a man who stirs up dissension among brothers. (Proverbs 6:16-19)

To fear the Lord is to hate evil; I hate pride and arrogance, evil behavior and perverse speech. (Proverbs 8:13)

When pride comes, then comes disgrace, but with humility comes wisdom. (Proverbs 11:2)

Pride only breeds quarrels, but wisdom is found in those who take advice. (Proverbs 13:10)

The Lord tears down the proud man's house but he keeps the widow's boundaries intact. (Proverbs 15:25)

The Lord detests all the proud of heart. Be sure of this: They will not go unpunished.

(Proverbs 16:5)

Pride goes before destruction, a haughty spirit before a fall. (Proverbs 16:18)

Before his downfall a man's heart is proud, but humility comes before honor. (Proverbs 18:12)

A haughty look, a proud heart, and the plowing of the wicked are sin. (Proverbs 21:4)

By humility and the fear of the Lord Are riches and honor and life. (Proverbs 22:4)

It is not good to eat too much honey, nor is it honorable to seek one's own honor. (Proverbs 25:27)

Do not boast about tomorrow, for you do not know what a day may bring forth. Let another praise you, and not your own mouth; someone else, and not your own lips. (Proverbs 27:1-2)

A man's pride will bring him low, but the humble in spirit will retain honor. (Proverbs 29:23)

The end of a matter is better than its beginning, and patience is better than pride. (Ecclesiastes 7:8)

The eyes of the arrogant man will be humbled and the pride of men brought low; the Lord alone will be exalted in that day. The Lord Almighty has a day in store for all the proud and lofty, for all that is exalted (and they will be humbled), (Isaiah 2:11-12)

The arrogance of man will be brought low and the pride of men humbled. (Isaiah 2:17)

I will punish the world for its evil, the wicked for their sins. I will put an end to the arrogance of the haughty and will humble the pride of the ruthless. (Isaiah 13:11)

You said in your heart, "I will ascend to heaven; I will raise my throne above the stars of God; I will sit enthroned on the mount of assembly, on the utmost heights of the sacred mountain. I will ascend above the tops of the clouds; I will make myself like the Most High." But you are brought down to the grave, to the depths of the pit. (Isaiah 14:13-15)

For this is what the High and lofty One says--he who lives forever, whose name is holy: "I live in a high and holy place, but also with him who is contrite and lowly in spirit, to revive the spirit of the lowly and to revive the heart of the contrite. (Isaiah 57:15)

This is the one I esteem: He who is humble and contrite in spirit, and trembles at my word. (Isaiah 66:2)

And they were haughty and committed abomination before Me; therefore, I took them away as I saw fit. (Ezekiel 16:50)

Read Daniel 4. King Nebuchadnezzar's pride resulted in a harsh punishment from God.

But when his heart became arrogant and hardened with pride, he was deposed from his royal throne and stripped of his glory. He was driven away from people and given the mind of an animal; he lived with the wild donkeys and ate grass like cattle; and his body was drenched with the dew of heaven, until he acknowledged that the Most High God is sovereign over the kingdoms of men and sets over them anyone he wishes. (Daniel 5:20-21)

"The pride of your heart has deceived you, you who live in the clefts of the rocks and make your home on the heights, you who say to yourself, 'Who can bring me down to the ground?' Though you soar like the eagle and make your nest among the stars, from there I will bring you down," declares the Lord. (Obadiah 3-4)

For whoever exalts himself will be humbled, and whoever humbles himself will be exalted. (Matthew 23:13)

He went on: "What comes out of a man is what makes him 'unclean.' For from within, out of men's hearts, come evil thoughts, sexual immorality, theft, murder, adultery, greed, malice, deceit, lewdness, envy, slander, arrogance and folly. All these evils come from inside and make a man 'unclean.'" (Mark 7:21-23)

He has scattered those who are proud in their inmost thoughts. He has brought down rulers from their thrones, but has lifted up the humble. (Luke 1:51-52)

For everyone who exalts himself will be humbled, and he who humbles himself will be exalted. (Luke 14:11)

So, you also, when you have done everything you were told to do, should say, "We are unworthy servants; we have only done our duty." (Luke 17:10)

To some who were confident of their own righteousness and looked down on everybody else, Jesus told this parable: "Two men went up to the temple to pray, one a Pharisee and the other a tax collector. The Pharisee stood up and prayed about himself: 'God, I thank you that I am not like other men--robbers, evildoers, adulterers--or even like this tax collector. I fast twice a week and give a tenth of all I get.' But the tax collector stood at a distance. He would not even look up to heaven, but beat his breast and said, 'God, have mercy on me, a sinner.' I tell you that this man, rather than the other, went home justified before God. For everyone who exalts himself will be humbled, and he who humbles himself will be exalted." (Luke 18:9-14)

For they loved praise from men more than praise from God. (John 12:43)

They are gossips, slanderers, God-haters, insolent, arrogant and boastful; they invent ways of doing evil; they disobey their parents; they are senseless, faithless, heartless, ruthless. Although they know God's righteous decree that those who do such things deserve death, they not only continue to do these very things but also approve of those who practice them. (Romans 1:30-32)

Do not think of yourself more highly than you ought, but rather think of yourself with sober judgment, in accordance with the measure of faith God has given you. (Romans 12:3)

Honor one another above yourselves. (Romans 12:10)

Do not be proud, but be willing to associate with people of low position. Do not be conceited. (Romans 12:16)

He chose the lowly things of this world and the despised things - and the things that are not - to nullify the things that are, so that no one may boast before him. (1 Corinthians 1:28-29)

Let him who boasts boast in the Lord. (1 Corinthians 1:31)

So, neither he who plants nor he who waters is anything, but only God, who makes things grow. (1 Corinthians 3:7)

For who makes you different from anyone else? What do you have that you did not receive? And if you did receive it, why do you boast as though you did not? (1 Corinthians 4:7)

But, let him who boasts boast in the Lord. For it is not the one who commends himself who is approved, but the one whom the Lord commends. (2 Corinthians 10:17-18)

Since we live by the Spirit, let us keep in step with the Spirit. Let us not become conceited, provoking and envying each other. (Galatians 5:25-26)

If anyone thinks he is something when he is nothing, he deceives himself. (Galatians 6:3)

Do nothing out of selfish ambition or vain conceit, but in humility consider others better than yourselves. (Philippians 2:3)

Your attitude should be the same as that of Christ Jesus: Who, being in very nature God, did not consider equality with God something to be grasped, but made himself nothing, taking the very nature of a servant, being made in human likeness. (Philippians 2:5-7)

But mark this: There will be terrible times in the last days. People will be lovers of themselves, lovers of money, boastful, proud, abusive, disobedient to their parents, ungrateful, unholy, without love, unforgiving, slanderous, without self-control, brutal, not lovers of the good, treacherous, rash, conceited, lovers of pleasure rather than lovers of God--having a form of godliness but denying its power. Have nothing to do with them. (2 Timothy 3:1-5)

But he gives us more grace. That is why Scripture says: "God opposes the proud but gives grace to the humble." (James 4:6)

Humble yourselves before the Lord, and he will lift you up. (James 4:10)

You boast and brag. All such boasting is evil. (James 4:16)

Young men, in the same way be submissive to those who are older. All of you, clothe yourselves with humility toward one another, because, "God opposes the proud but gives grace to the humble." Humble yourselves, therefore, under God's mighty hand, that he may lift you up in due time. (1 Peter 5:5-6)

For everything in the world--the cravings of sinful man, the lust of his eyes and the boasting of what he has and does--comes not from the Father but from the world. The world and its desires pass away, but the man who does the will of God lives forever. (1 John 2:16-17)

CHAPTER FIVE

The "it" of Weakness

DEFINITION: Weakness is a condition of being fatigued, tired, and inadequate physically, mentally, spiritually, or emotionally to the extent that you cannot function effectively.

FACTS ABOUT WEAKNESS:

There are two main types of weakness. One is weakness (as defined above) that hinders you from functioning effectively. The other type of weakness is desiring something so much that you are unable to resist it. The latter meaning is dealt with as "Temptation" in this database.

Weakness is multi-faceted and interrelated. You can experience physical, mental, spiritual, or emotional weakness. One type of weakness can affect other areas of your life. For example, emotional weakness can also affect your physical body by causing stress.

What causes weakness. Spiritual weakness is caused by not spending time with God and in His Word and/or refusing to do God's revealed will. Emotional weakness can result from not dealing properly with difficult circumstances and wrong emotional responses. Physical weakness results from sickness, lack of exercise, or lack of proper rest. Mental weakness results from not controlling your thought life. (Mental weakness, as defined here, does not mean mental illness. See "Mental Illness" in this database for coverage of this topic.) Weakness can also result from receiving the Lord's Supper improperly (1 Corinthians 11:28-30).

DEALING WITH WEAKNESS:

Analyze your weakness. It is important to discover the root cause of your weakness so you can deal with it and not repeat behaviors that are causing it. Are you experiencing physical weakness resulting from an illness or not eating, resting, or exercising? Is it emotional weakness due to not handling negative circumstances properly? Is it spiritual weakness resulting from lack of time with God, in prayer, and in the Word? Are you losing the spiritual battle for you mind? Are you deliberately disobeying God and doing something that is causing spiritual, mental, emotional, or physical weakness?

Admit your weakness to God. The Apostle Paul admitted his weakness to God, and in so doing God gave him strength (2 Corinthians 12:8-10). Sometimes God supernaturally eliminates your weakness, but at other times He gives you strength in the midst of it.

Accept and confess God's provision for strength in your weakness. The same spirit that raised Christ from the dead dwells within you. Draw upon that strength. Claim promises like Philippians 4:13: *"I can do everything through him who gives me strength."*

Correct root causes of your weakness. If your weakness is physical because of improper rest, exercise, or diet, correct these. If you have been losing the battle for your mind, study the topic of the "Mind and Thoughts" in this database. If you are emotionally weak, learn how to handle your emotions properly. Correct any sinful behaviors that may be causing weakness. For sure, spend time with God and His Word to strengthen yourself spiritually.

Spend time in God's presence. *"But those who wait on the Lord shall renew their strength; they shall mount up with wings like eagles, they shall run and not be weary, they shall walk and not faint" (Isaiah 40:31, NKJV).*

Recognize that when you are weak, you are strong spiritually. Weaknesses, handicaps, and inadequacies can be positive in that they make you recognize your dependence on God. This relieves you of trying to do God's work in your own strength, and motivates you to function in the power of the Holy Spirit. It replaces pride with humbleness and provides a marvelous opportunity for the Lord to demonstrate what He can do through you. Weakness actually attracts God's strength (2 Corinthians 12:8-10).

WHAT GOD'S WORD SAYS ABOUT WEAKNESS:

...Your strength will equal your days. (Deuteronomy 33:25)

Look to the Lord and his strength; seek his face always. (1 Chronicles 16:11)

But as for you, be strong and do not give up, for your work will be rewarded. (2 Chronicles 15:7)

...for the joy of the Lord is your strength. (Nehemiah 8:10)

The Lord is my rock and my fortress and my deliverer; My God, my strength, in whom I will trust; My shield and the horn of my salvation, my stronghold. (Psalms 18:2, NKJV)

He reached down from on high and took hold of me; he drew me out of deep waters. He rescued me from my powerful enemy, from my foes, who were too strong for me. (Psalm 18:16-17)

You give me your shield of victory, and your right hand sustains me; you stoop down to make me great. (Psalm 18:35)

You armed me with strength for battle; you made my adversaries bow at my feet. (Psalms 18:39)

The Lord is my light and my salvation; Whom shall I fear? The Lord is the strength of my life; Of whom shall I be afraid? (Psalms 27:1, NKJV)

The Lord is my strength and my shield; my heart trusts in him, and I am helped. My heart leaps for joy and I will give thanks to him in song. (Psalms 28:7)

The Lord gives strength to his people; the Lord blesses his people with peace. (Psalms 29:1)

Be strong and take heart, all you who hope in the Lord. (Psalm 31:24)

But the salvation of the righteous is from the Lord; He is their strength in the time of trouble. And the Lord shall help them and deliver them; He shall deliver them from the wicked, and save them, because they trust in Him. (Psalms 37:39-40, NKJV)

God is our refuge and strength, an ever-present help in trouble. (Psalm 46:1)

My soul finds rest in God alone; my salvation comes from him. (Psalm 62:1)

My flesh and my heart may fail, but God is the strength of my heart and my portion forever. (Psalm 73:26)

Look to the Lord and his strength; seek his face always. (Psalm 105:4)

The Lord is my strength and my song; he has become my salvation. (Psalm 118:14)

The Lord upholds all those who fall and lifts up all who are bowed down. (Psalm 145:14)

Surely God is my salvation; I will trust and not be afraid. The Lord, the Lord, is my strength and my song; he has become my salvation. (Isaiah 12:2)

For thus said the Lord God, the Holy one of Israel: In returning [to Me] and resting [in Me] you shall be saved; in quietness and in [trusting] confidence shall be your strength. But you would not, (Isaiah 30:15, AMP)

He gives strength to the weary, and increases the power of the weak. (Isaiah 40:29)

But those who wait on the Lord Shall renew their strength; they shall mount up with wings like eagles, they shall run and not be weary, they shall walk and not faint. (Isaiah 40:31, NKJV)

So do not fear, for I am with you; do not be dismayed, for I am your God. I will strengthen you and help you; I will uphold you with my righteous right hand. (Isaiah 41:10)

"Come to me, all you who are weary and burdened, and I will give you rest. Take my yoke upon you and learn from me, for I am gentle and humble in heart, and you will find rest for your souls. For my yoke is easy and my burden is light." (Matthew 11:28-30)

For the foolishness of God is wiser than man's wisdom, and the weakness of God is stronger than man's strength. (1 Corinthians 1:25)

God chose the weak things of the world to shame the strong. (1 Corinthians 1:27)

A man ought to examine himself before he eats of the bread and drinks of the cup. For anyone who eats and drinks without recognizing the body of the Lord eats and drinks judgment on himself. That is why many among you are weak and sick, and a number of you have fallen asleep. (1 Corinthians 11:28-30)

The body that is sown is perishable, it is raised imperishable; it is sown in dishonor, it is raised in glory; it is sown in weakness, it is raised in power; it is sown a natural body, it is raised a spiritual body. (1 Corinthians 15:42-44)

But he said to me, "My grace is sufficient for you, for my power is made perfect in weakness." Therefore, I will boast all the more gladly about my weaknesses, so that Christ's power may rest on me. That is why, for Christ's sake, I delight in weaknesses, in insults, in hardships, in persecutions, in difficulties. For when I am weak, then I am strong. (2 Corinthians 12:9-10)

Let us not become weary in doing good, for at the proper time we will reap a harvest if we do not give up. (Galatians 6:9)

Finally, my brethren, be strong in the Lord and in the power of His might. (Ephesians 6:10, NKJV)

I can do everything through him who gives me strength. (Philippians 4:13)

To this end I labor, struggling with all his energy, which so powerfully works in me. (Colossians 1:29)

And what more shall I say? I do not have time to tell about Gideon, Barak, Samson, Jephthah, David, Samuel and the prophets, who through faith conquered kingdoms, administered justice, and gained what was promised; who shut the mouths of lions, quenched the fury of the flames, and escaped the edge of the sword; whose weakness was turned to strength; and who became powerful in battle and routed foreign armies. (Hebrews 11:32-34)

CHAPTER SIX

The "it" of Covetousness

DEFINITION: Covetousness is a driving desire to have that which one does not possess, control, have access to, use of, or authority over.

FACTS ABOUT COVETEOUSNESS:

Covetousness is sin. The Bible declares: *"You shall not covet your neighbor's house. You shall not covet your neighbor's wife, or his manservant or maidservant, his ox or donkey, or anything that belongs to your neighbor" (Exodus 20:17).*

Covetousness results from a love of the world. The Bible warns: *"Do not love the world or the things in the world. If anyone loves the world, the love of the Father is not in him. For all that is in the world--the lust of the flesh, the lust of the eyes, and the pride of life--is not of the Father but is of the world. And the world is passing away, and the lust of it; but he who does the will of God abides forever" (1 John 2:15-17, NKJV).*

Covetousness comes from your heart. Jesus said: *"For from within, out of the heart of men, proceed evil thoughts, adulteries, fornications, murders, Thefts, covetousness, wickedness, deceit, lasciviousness, an evil eye, blasphemy, pride, foolishness: All these evil things come from within, and defile the man" (Mark 7:21-33, KJV).*

DEALING WITH COVETEOUSNESS:

Ask God to forgive your covetousness. Covetousness is sin, and as all sin, confession and repentance is required.

Ask God to change your heart. Covetousness comes from the heart. Pray the prayer of the psalmist: *"Turn my heart toward your statutes and not toward selfish gain" (Psalm 119:36)*

Ask God to help you order your priorities. Make spiritual things your desire and priority instead of coveting after carnal things: *"So do not worry, saying, 'What shall we eat?' or 'What shall we drink?' or 'What shall we wear?' For the pagans run after all these things, and your heavenly Father knows that you need them. But seek first his kingdom and his righteousness, and all these things will be given to you as well" (Matthew 6:31-33).*

WHAT GOD'S WORD SAYS ABOUT COVETEOUSNESS:

You shall not covet your neighbor's house. You shall not covet your neighbor's wife, or his manservant or maidservant, his ox or donkey, or anything that belongs to your neighbor. (Exodus 20:17).

Turn my heart toward your statutes and not toward selfish gain. (Psalm 119:36)

So, do not worry, saying, 'What shall we eat?' or 'What shall we drink?' or 'What shall we wear?'
For the pagans run after all these things, and your heavenly Father knows that you need them.
But seek first his kingdom and his righteousness, and all these things will be given to you as
well. (Matthew 6:31-33)

For from within, out of the heart of men, proceed evil thoughts, adulteries, fornications, murders,
Thefts, covetousness, wickedness, deceit, lasciviousness, an evil eye, blasphemy, pride,
foolishness: All these evil things come from within, and defile the man. (Mark 7:21-33, KJV)

For the love of money is the root of all evil: which while some coveted after, they have erred
from the faith, and pierced themselves through with many sorrows. But thou, O man of God, flee
these things; and follow after righteousness, godliness, faith, love, patience, meekness. (1
Timothy 6:10-11, KJV)

Let your conversation be without covetousness; and be content with such things as ye have: for
he has said, I will never leave thee, nor forsake thee. (Hebrews 13:5, KJV)

What causes fights and quarrels among you? Don't they come from your desires that battle
within you? You want something but don't get it. You kill and covet, but you cannot have what
you want. You quarrel and fight. You do not have, because you do not ask God. When you ask,
you do not receive, because you ask with wrong motives, that you may spend what you get on
your pleasures. (James 4:1-3)

Do not love the world or the things in the world. If anyone loves the world, the love of the Father
is not in him. For all that is in the world--the lust of the flesh, the lust of the eyes, and the pride
of life--is not of the Father but is of the world. And the world is passing away, and the lust of it;
but he who does the will of God abides forever. (1 John 2:15-17, NKJV)

CHAPTER SEVEN

The "it" of Rebellion to Authority

DEFINITION: An authority is someone who is set over you in a structured environment for specific purposes. Examples are your boss in the workplace, your spiritual leader, the government of your nation, and law enforcement officials.

FACTS ABOUT AUTHORITY:

You are set free in Christ, but still under authority. Christ sets you free from sin, guilt, and condemnation, but not from God's authority and the authorities ordained by God.

Authority provides positive structure. In the home, community, church, the workplace, and government, authority provides structure within which you can live your life confidently.

All authority is from God. When you rebel against legitimate authority, you rebel against God: *"Everyone must submit himself to the governing authorities, for there is no authority except that which God has established. The authorities that exist have been established by God. Consequently, he who rebels against the authority is rebelling against what God has instituted, and those who do so will bring judgment on themselves" (Romans 13:1-3).*

DEALING WITH AUTHORITY:

You must obey authorities. Because all authority is from God, you are to obey instead of rebel. When you rebel against them, you rebel against God Himself (Romans 13:1-3).

When authorities conflict with God's Word, you must obey God. When ordered to no longer preach about Christ, Peter responded: *"We must obey God rather than men!" (Acts 5:29).*

Pray for those in authority. *"I urge, then, first of all, that requests, prayers, intercession and thanksgiving be made for everyone--for kings and all those in authority, that we may live peaceful and quiet lives in all godliness and holiness" (1 Timothy 2:1-2).*

Respect the authority set in the church. Guidelines for functioning under authority in the church are given in 1 Corinthians 12:28; Ephesians 4:11-12; and Hebrews 13:17. If you cannot respect the leadership in a church because of their ungodly conduct, find a new church!

Respect the structure of authority set in the home. A godly husband is to be the head of the house, the wife is to follow his lead, and children are to be obedient. The authority in the home is to be loving and kind, not demanding and harsh.

Lovingly exercise authority over those for whom you are responsible. As a parent, spouse, pastor, employer, or public servant, you are to loving exercise our authority in a Christ-like attitude: *"Submit to one another out of reverence for Christ" (Ephesians 5:21).*

WHAT GOD'S WORD SAYS ABOUT AUTHORITY:

Everyone must submit himself to the governing authorities, for there is no authority except that which God has established. The authorities that exist have been established by God. Consequently, he who rebels against the authority is rebelling against what God has instituted, and those who do so will bring judgment on themselves. (Romans 13:1-3)

Submit to one another out of reverence for Christ. (Ephesians 5:21)

I urge, then, first of all, that requests, prayers, intercession and thanksgiving be made for everyone--for kings and all those in authority, that we may live peaceful and quiet lives in all godliness and holiness. (1 Timothy 2:1-2)

Obey your leaders and submit to their authority. They keep watch over you as men who must give an account. Obey them so that their work will be a joy, not a burden, for that would be of no advantage to you. (Hebrews 13:17)

Submit yourselves for the Lord's sake to every authority instituted among men: whether to the king, as the supreme authority, or to governors, who are sent by him to punish those who do wrong and to commend those who do right. For it is God's will that by doing good you should silence the ignorant talk of foolish men. (1 Peter 2:13-15)

CHAPTER EIGHT

The "it" of Disobedience

DEFINITION: Disobedience is refusing to follow instructions and to comply with rules or regulations. Biblically, disobedience is refusing to obey God, the commands in His Word, and leaders who have God-given authority over you.

FACTS ABOUT DISOBEDIENCE:

Disobedience is sin. Biblical, disobedience is not "exercising your right to choose" or "freedom of choice". It is sin. Obedience is the opposite of disobedience. Obedience is acceptance and submission to the authority of God and His Word.

God expects obedience. Your entire relationship with Him is based on obedience, beginning with your obedience in accepting Jesus as Savior (Deuteronomy 11:26-28).

Disobedience will prevent you from taking possession of the promises of God. It kept an entire nation out of their promised land. When Israel disobeyed God, they were sent back into the wilderness to wander for forty years (Nehemiah 9:17).

Disobedience includes sins of commission--things you should have done and did not do--and sins of commission--sinful acts you committed contrary to God's Word.

You are required to obey authorities. It is a command: *"Obey your leaders and submit to their authority" (Hebrews 13:17).*

Strategies of Satan that will lead you into disobedience.
    -He causes you to doubt God and His Word.
    -He tempts you to murmur against God.
    -He causes you to turn away from God.
    -He causes you to reject God's voice and His Word.
    -He causes you to no longer fear God.
    -He causes you to fear man more than you fear God.
    -He causes you to reject God's will and follow your own plan.
    -He deceives you into compromising.

DEALING WITH DISOBEDIENCE:

Repent of your disobedience. Disobedience is sin, and as with any sin you must confess it and ask forgiveness from God.

Determine you will obey God. You have the power to obey God. Sin no longer has dominion over you: *"For sin shall not [any longer] exert dominion over you, since now you are not under Law [as slaves], but under grace [as subjects of God's favor and mercy]." (Romans 6:14 AMP)*

Practice obedience in routine decisions.   Then you will develop the habit of obeying and will not fail to obey God in the big decisions of life.

WHAT GOD'S WORD SAYS ABOUT DISOBEDIENCE:

Oh, that their hearts would be inclined to fear me and keep all my commands always, so that it might go well with them and their children forever! (Deuteronomy 5:29)

See, I am setting before you today a blessing and a curse--the blessing if you obey the commands of the Lord your God that I am giving you today; the curse if you disobey the commands of the Lord your God and turn from the way that I command you today by following other gods, which you have not known. (Deuteronomy 11:26-28)

It is the Lord your God you must follow, and him you must revere. Keep his commands and obey him; serve him and hold fast to him. (Deuteronomy 13:4)

This day I call heaven and earth as witnesses against you that I have set before you life and death, blessings and curses. Now choose life, so that you and your children may live and that you may love the Lord your God, listen to his voice, and hold fast to him. For the Lord is your life... (Deuteronomy 30:19-20)

Do not let this Book of the Law depart from your mouth; meditate on it day and night, so that you may be careful to do everything written in it. Then you will be prosperous and successful. Have I not commanded you? Be strong and courageous. Do not be terrified; do not be discouraged, for the Lord your God will be with you wherever you go. (Joshua 1:8-9)

If you fear the Lord and serve and obey him and do not rebel against his commands, and if both you and the king who reigns over you follow the Lord your God--good! But if you do not obey the Lord, and if you rebel against his commands, his hand will be against you, as it was against your fathers. (1 Samuel 12:14-15)

But Samuel replied: "Does the Lord delight in burnt offerings and sacrifices as much as in obeying the voice of the Lord? To obey is better than sacrifice, and to heed is better than the fat of rams. For rebellion is like the sin of divination, and arrogance like the evil of idolatry."
(1 Samuel 15:22-23)

Blessed are they whose ways are blameless, who walk according to the law of the Lord. (Psalm 119:1)

Streams of tears flow from my eyes, for your law is not obeyed. (Psalm 119:136)

I look on the faithless with loathing, for they do not obey your word. (Psalm 119:158)

I obey your statutes, for I love them greatly. (Psalm 119:167)

He who obeys instructions guards his life, but he who is contemptuous of his ways will die. (Proverbs 19:16)

If you are willing and obedient, you will eat the best from the land; but if you resist and rebel, you will be devoured by the sword." For the mouth of the Lord has spoken. (Isaiah 1:19)

Walk in all the ways I command you, that it may go well with you. (Jeremiah 7:23)

Obey me and do everything I command you, and you will be my people, and I will be your God. (Jeremiah 11:4)

See how each of you is following the stubbornness of his evil heart instead of obeying me. (Jeremiah 16:12)

Not everyone who says to me, 'Lord, Lord,' will enter the kingdom of heaven, but only he who does the will of my Father who is in heaven. Many will say to me on that day, 'Lord, Lord, did we not prophesy in your name and in your name, drive out demons and perform many miracles?' Then I will tell them plainly, 'I never knew you. Away from me, you evildoers!' Therefore, everyone who hears these words of mine and puts them into practice is like a wise man who built his house on the rock. The rain came down, the streams rose, and the winds blew and beat against that house; yet it did not fall, because it had its foundation on the rock. But everyone who hears these words of mine and does not put them into practice is like a foolish man who built his house on sand. The rain came down, the streams rose, and the winds blew and beat against that house, and it fell with a great crash. (Matthew 7:21-24)

Why do you call me, 'Lord, Lord,' and do not do what I say? (Luke 6:46)

If you love me, you will obey what I command. (John 14:15)

Jesus replied, "If anyone loves me, he will obey my teaching. My Father will love him, and we will come to him and make our home with him. He who does not love me will not obey my teaching. These words you hear are not my own; they belong to the Father who sent me." (John 14:23-24)

If you obey my commands, you will remain in my love, just as I have obeyed my Father's commands and remain in his love. (John 15:10)

We must obey God rather than men! (Acts 5:29)

For just as through the disobedience of the one man the many were made sinners, so also through the obedience of the one man the many will be made righteous. (Romans 5:19)

Therefore, do not let sin reign in your mortal body so that you obey its evil desires. Do not offer the parts of your body to sin, as instruments of wickedness, but rather offer yourselves to God, as those who have been brought from death to life; and offer the parts of your body to him as instruments of righteousness. For sin shall not be your master, because you are not under law, but under grace. (Romans 6:12-14)

Don't you know that when you offer yourselves to someone to obey him as slaves, you are slaves to the one whom you obey--whether you are slaves to sin, which leads to death, or to obedience, which leads to righteousness? But thanks be to God that, though you used to be slaves to sin, you wholeheartedly obeyed the form of teaching to which you were entrusted. You have been set free from sin and have become slaves to righteousness. (Romans 6:16-18)

We demolish arguments and every pretension that sets itself up against the knowledge of God, and we take captive every thought to make it obedient to Christ. And we will be ready to punish every act of disobedience, once your obedience is complete. (2 Corinthians 10:5-6)

You were running a good race. Who cut in on you and kept you from obeying the truth? (Galatians 5:7)

Let no one deceive you with empty words, for because of such things God's wrath comes on those who are disobedient. Therefore, do not be partners with them. (Ephesians 5:6-7)

Children, obey your parents in the Lord, for this is right. "Honor your father and mother"-which is the first commandment with a promise "that it may go well with you and that you may enjoy long life on the earth." (Ephesians 6:1-3)

Children, obey your parents in everything, for this pleases the Lord. (Colossians 3:20)

Slaves, obey your earthly masters in everything; and do it, not only when their eye is on you and to win their favor, but with sincerity of heart and reverence for the Lord. Whatever you do, work at it with all your heart, as working for the Lord, not for men, since you know that you will receive an inheritance from the Lord as a reward. It is the Lord Christ you are serving (Colossians 3:22-24)

Remind the people to be subject to rulers and authorities, to be obedient, to be ready to do whatever is good, to slander no one, to be peaceable and considerate, and to show true humility toward all men. (Titus 3:1-2)

Obey your leaders and submit to their authority. They keep watch over you as men who must give an account. Obey them so that their work will be a joy, not a burden, for that would be of no advantage to you. (Hebrews 13:17)

Anyone who listens to the word but does not do what it says is like a man who looks at his face in a mirror and, after looking at himself, goes away and immediately forgets what he looks like.

But the man who looks intently into the perfect law that gives freedom, and continues to do this, not forgetting what he has heard, but doing it – he will be blessed in what he does. (James 1:23-25)

We know that we have come to know him if we obey his commands. (1 John 2:3)

This is how we know we are in him: Whoever claims to live in him must walk as Jesus did. (1 John 2:5-6)

Those who obey his commands live in him, and he in them. (1 John 3:24)

This is how we know that we love the children of God: by loving God and carrying out his commands. This is love for God: to obey his commands. And his commands are not burdensome, for everyone born of God overcomes the world. (1 John 5:2-4)

Anyone who runs ahead and does not continue in the teaching of Christ does not have God; whoever continues in the teaching has both the Father and the Son. (2 John 1:9)

Remember, therefore, what you have received and heard; obey it, and repent. (Revelation 3:3)

CHAPTER NINE

The "it" of Fear

DEFINITION: Fear is a sense of alarm or apprehension of danger. For a believer, fear is an expression of unbelief in God or a lack of understanding of His ways.

FACTS ABOUT FEAR:

All fear is not bad. The "fight or flight" response that is common to all people is not negative. "Fight or flight" is a normal response that protects you in the face of perceived danger. For example, if you are threatened by a dangerous beast your "fight or flight" response will kick in so you can either escape or successfully confront the animal. This is a rational response to danger that differs from irrational and tormenting fears.

Fear was first manifested when Adam and Eve sinned in the Garden of Eden. When God came seeking them in the cool of the day, Adam replied: "...*I heard your voice in the garden, and I was afraid...*" *(Genesis 3:10).* One of the first negative emotions resulting from sin was fear.

Fear is a spirit. The Bible declares that God has not given us the spirit of fear (2 Timothy 1:7). If the spirit of fear is not from God, then it is from Satan.

Fear is a tormenting emotion According to 1 John 4:18, fear has torment.

Fear fosters irrational phobias and negative emotions. It's most severe manifestations cause's people to withdraw from society and become agoraphobics--confined in their own home where they think they are safe. The spirit of fear will make you a slave to fear (Romans 8:15-16).

Medical science has proven that fear results in stress, high blood pressure, strokes, and heart attacks. The Bible speaks of men's hearts failing because of fear (Luke 21:26) and of people living in bondage all of their lives because of the fear of death (Hebrews 2:15).

Fear is sin and leads to other sins. You are either functioning in fear or in faith, and whatever is not of faith is sin (Romans 14:23). There are numerous biblical examples of fear leading to additional sins. Abraham was so afraid of Abimelech that he lied to save his own life, saying Sarah was his sister (Genesis 20:1-13). Isaac feared for his life and committed the same sin (Genesis 26:7). Ten of the twelve spies who investigated the promised land were terrified of the giants and their fear resulted in Israel's disobedience and the death of a whole generation (Numbers 13). Saul tried to murder David because he feared him (1 Samuel 18:12,15,29) and later Saul sinned by offering a burnt offering because he feared the people would scatter (1 Samuel 13:11-12). Acting in fear cost Saul the kingdom. What will fear cost you?

Fear focuses on the future--whether it be today, tomorrow, or in the distant future. God designed the universe to run on a 24-hour period of time. That is why the prayer Jesus taught

His disciples was to be a daily prayer for needs to be provided, forgiveness, etc. Fear enters in when you violate this principle and begin to worry about the future (Matthew 6:25-34).

DEALING WITH FEAR:

Ask yourself, "Why am I so fearful?" Jesus asked His disciples this question (Mark 4:40).

Deal with fear spiritually. Because most fear is irrational, it cannot be dealt with through rational means. Fear must be dealt with spiritually. David said: *"I sought the Lord, and he answered me; he delivered me from all my fears" (Psalm 34:4).*

Repent of fear. Whatever is not of faith is sin (Romans 14:23). Fear is not faith, so it is sin. When you fear, you are functioning in unbelief--not trusting God to care for you and your concerns,

Make your fears a matter of prayer. When David sought the Lord, he was delivered from all of his fears (Psalm 34:4). Philippians 4:6-7 directs us to make every concern a matter of prayer instead of worrying, and we will function in God's peace instead of fear.

Focus on God instead of the fear. Isaiah 26:3 promises: *"You will keep in perfect peace him whose mind is steadfast, because he trusts in you."* David said he sought the Lord, and He delivered him from all of His fear (Psalm 34:4).

Do not fear the future. Claim God's promise instead: *"For I know the plans I have for you," declares the Lord, "plans to prosper you and not to harm you, plans to give you hope and a future" (Jeremiah 29:11).*

Eliminate things that feed your fear. These include scare tactics generated by others and media violence viewed through news reports, horror movies, the Internet, or violent video games.

Overcome fear by God's power, His love, and a sound mind. These are the keys given in 2 Timothy 1:7: *"For God has not given us a spirit of fear, but of power and of love and of a sound mind".* You overcome fear by:

> *-Power*. Jesus delegated to believer's power over all the power of the enemy (Luke 10:19). Face your fears in the power of the promises of God.

> *-Love*. You eliminate fear by really coming to understand the love of God. His perfect love casts out fear (1 John 4:16-18).

> *-A sound mind.* Irrational fear is just that: Not rational. It is the result of irrational thinking, so you cannot deal with fear by trying to be rational. You must develop a sound mind that cannot be tormented by fear (Romans 12:1-2). You do this by living by the Spirit rather than by the flesh (Romans 8:5-6).   Fear begins in the mind, and it is in the mind where you must conquer it. Fear is a battle that starts with lies instigated by the

god of this world and the father of lies, Satan (John 8:44). This is why the scriptures direct you to cast down vain imaginations. "Cast down" means to conquer, pull down, and hold under one's power. The word "imaginations" means logic. Your mind can develop strongholds that result from logical reasoning. A sound mind is one controlled by the Holy Spirit, rather than the logic of your own carnal mind.

Do not play the "what if" game. "What if this happens, what if that happens?" The power to face difficult situations is given when it is needed, not when you are worrying over the future (Hebrews 4:15-16).

Reject the fear of death. The fear of death is a major issue for many people (Hebrews 2:15). True believers need not fear death, because when you vacate your body you will immediately be in the presence of the Lord (1 Corinthians 6:8). The Apostle Paul said that to die would be gain (Philippians 1:21). Peter refers to death as putting off an earthly tabernacle (2 Peter 1:14). David wrote: *"Even though I walk through the valley of the shadow of death, I will fear no evil, for you are with me; your rod and your staff, they comfort me " (Psalm 23:4).* When Jesus returns, you will be reunited with your loved ones (1 Thessalonians 4:13-18).

Make this declaration daily. *"What time I am afraid, I will trust in thee. In God I will praise his word, in God I have put my trust; I will not fear what flesh can do unto me...In God have I put my trust: I will not be afraid what man can do unto me" (Psalm 56:3-4,11).*

Be of good courage. Courage is not the absence of fear, rather it is acting and persevering in spite of fear. God repeatedly told His people to be of good courage (Deuteronomy 31:6-7,23; Joshua 1:6,9,18; Joshua 10:25; 1 Chronicles 28:20).   The psalmist said if you wait on the Lord and are of good courage you will receive the strength you need to face the difficulties of life (Psalm 27:14; 32:24).

Praise the Lord in the face of fear. David did so and God delivered him from all of his fears (Psalm 34:1-4).

WHAT GOD'S WORD SAYS ABOUT FEAR:

The Bible is filled with references about fear--so many that we cannot include them all. Use a concordance to study the subject of "fear" in the Bible. Here are some key selected references.

Moses answered the people, "Do not be afraid. Stand firm and you will see the deliverance the Lord will bring you today." (Exodus 14:13)

Have I not commanded you? Be strong and courageous. Do not be terrified; do not be discouraged, for the Lord your God will be with you wherever you go. (Joshua 1:9)

"Don't be afraid," the prophet answered. "Those who are with us are more than those who are with them." (2 Kings 6:16)

Even though I walk through the valley of the shadow of death, I will fear no evil, for you are with me; your rod and your staff, they comfort me. (Psalm 23:4)

The Lord is my light and my salvation--whom shall I fear? The Lord is the stronghold of my life --of whom shall I be afraid? (Psalm 27:1)

I will extol the Lord at all times; his praise will always be on my lips. My soul will boast in the Lord; let the afflicted hear and rejoice. Glorify the Lord with me; let us exalt his name together. I sought the Lord, and he answered me; he delivered me from all my fears.
(Psalm 34:1-4)

Therefore we will not fear, though the earth give way and the mountains fall into the heart of the sea, though its waters roar and foam and the mountains quake with their surging. (Psalm 46:2-3)

When I am afraid, I will trust in you. In God, whose word I praise, in God I trust; I will not be afraid. What can mortal man do to me? When I am afraid, I will trust in you. (Psalm 56:3-4)

You will not fear the terror of night, nor the arrow that flies by day, nor the pestilence that stalks in the darkness, nor the plague that destroys at midday. A thousand may fall at your side, ten thousand at your right hand, but it will not come near you. (Psalm 91:5-7)

The Lord is with me; I will not be afraid. What can man do to me? (Psalm 118:6)

The Lord watches over all who love him. (Psalm 145:20)

...but whoever listens to me will live in safety and be at ease, without fear of harm.
(Proverbs 1:33)

The wicked man flees though no one pursues, but the righteous are as bold as a lion.
(Proverbs 28:1)

Fear of man will prove to be a snare, but whoever trusts in the Lord is kept safe. (Proverbs 29:25)

Surely God is my salvation; I will trust and not be afraid. (Isaiah 12:2)

You will keep in perfect peace him whose mind is steadfast, because he trusts in you.
(Isaiah 26:3)

Strengthen the feeble hands, steady the knees that give way; say to those with fearful hearts, "Be strong, do not fear, your God will come." (Isaiah 35:3-4)

So do not fear, for I am with you; do not be dismayed, for I am your God. I will strengthen you and help you; I will uphold you with my righteous right hand. (Isaiah 41:10)

But now, this is what the Lord says--he who created you, O Jacob, he who formed you, O Israel:
"Fear not, for I have redeemed you; I have summoned you by name; you are mine.
When you pass through the waters, I will be with you; and when you pass through the rivers,
they will not sweep over you. When you walk through the fire, you will not be burned;
the flames will not set you ablaze." (Isaiah 43:1-2)

"For I know the plans I have for you," declares the Lord, "plans to prosper you and not to harm
you, plans to give you hope and a future." (Jeremiah 29:11)

So, do not worry, saying, 'What shall we eat?' or 'What shall we drink?' or 'What shall we wear?'
For the pagans run after all these things, and your heavenly Father knows that you need them.
But seek first his kingdom and his righteousness, and all these things will be given to you as
well. Therefore, do not worry about tomorrow, for tomorrow will worry about itself. Each day
has enough trouble of its own. (Matthew 6:31-34)

You of little faith, why are you so afraid? (Matthew 8:26)

Do not be afraid of those who kill the body but cannot kill the soul. Rather, be afraid of the One
who can destroy both soul and body in hell. Are not two sparrows sold for a penny? Yet not one
of them will fall to the ground apart from the will of your Father. And even the very hairs of
your head are all numbered. So, don't be afraid; you are worth more than many sparrows.
(Matthew 10:28-31)

Don't be afraid; just believe. (Mark 5:36)

I have given you authority to trample on snakes and scorpions and to overcome all the power of
the enemy; nothing will harm you. (Luke 10:19)

Do not be afraid, little flock, for your Father has been pleased to give you the kingdom. (Luke
12:32)

Peace I leave with you; My [own] peace I now give and bequeath to you. Not as the world gives
do I give to you. Do not let your hearts be troubled, neither let them be afraid. [Stop allowing
yourselves to be agitated and disturbed; and do not permit yourselves to be fearful and
intimidated and cowardly and unsettled.] (John 14:27, AMP)

For you did not receive a spirit that makes you a slave again to fear, but you received the Spirit
of sonship. And by him we cry, "Abba, Father." The Spirit himself testifies with our spirit that
we are God's children. (Romans 8:15-16)

... everything that does not come from faith is sin. (Romans 14:23)

Stand firm in one spirit, contending as one man for the faith of the gospel, without being
frightened in any way by those who oppose you. (Philippians 1:27-28)

Do not be anxious about anything, but in everything, by prayer and petition, with thanksgiving, present your requests to God. And the peace of God, which transcends all understanding, will guard your hearts and your minds in Christ Jesus. (Philippians 4:6-7)

For God has not given us a spirit of fear, but of power and of love and of a sound mind. (2 Timothy 1:7)

Since the children have flesh and blood, he (Jesus) too shared in their humanity so that by his death he might destroy him who holds the power of death--that is, the devil--and free those who all their lives were held in slavery by their fear of death. (Hebrews 2:14-15).

For we do not have a high priest who is unable to sympathize with our weaknesses, but we have one who has been tempted in every way, just as we are--yet was without sin. Let us then approach the throne of grace with confidence, so that we may receive mercy and find grace to help us in our time of need. (Hebrews 4:15-16).

The Lord is my helper; I will not be afraid. (Hebrews 13:6)

You are of God, little children, and have overcome them, because He who is in you is greater than he who is in the world. (1 John 4:4, NKJV)

There is no fear in love; but perfect love casts out fear, because fear involves torment. But he who fears has not been made perfect in love. (1 John 1:18, NKJV)

Do not be afraid of what you are about to suffer. I tell you, the devil will put some of you in prison to test you, and you will suffer persecution for ten days. Be faithful, even to the point of death, and I will give you the crown of life. (Revelation 2:10)

CHAPTER TEN

The "it of Persecution

DEFINITION: Persecution is the act of subjecting someone to cruel and unfair treatment because of their ethnic origin, political views, or religious beliefs. The biblical definition includes harassing, punishing, oppressing, or even killing those who serve God and refuse to deny Him.

FACTS ABOUT PERSECUTION:

The targets of persecution. The Bible reveals that true believers--those who proclaim God's Word and live by His commandments--are the targets of persecution.

All who live godly will suffer persecution. The Apostle Paul warned*: "In fact, everyone who wants to live a godly life in Christ Jesus will be persecuted" (2 Timothy 3: 12).*

Reasons for persecution include misunderstanding, jealousy, revenge, opposition, hatred of God and His Word, and Satanically-inspired motives.

The root causes of persecution in a biblical sense are wicked men who are motivated by Satanic powers to oppose God, His Word, all that is good, and believers who choose to follow the Lord. The world hates believers because they are not of this world (John 17:14-18).

You are actually blessed when you are persecuted. Matthew 5:11-12 says: *"Blessed are you when people insult you, persecute you and falsely say all kinds of evil against you because of me. Rejoice and be glad, because great is your reward in heaven, for in the same way they persecuted the prophets who were before you."*

DEALING WITH PERSECUTION:

Pray that you will be delivered from persecution. "Deliver us from evil" is part of the model prayer (Matthew 6:13). Paul said to *"...pray that we may be delivered from wicked and evil men, for not everyone has faith" (2 Thessalonians 3:2).* David prayed *"save and deliver me from all who pursue me" (Psalm 7:1).*

Forgive those who persecute you. You must extend to those who persecute you the same forgiveness that you have received (Matthew 6:12).

Love those who persecute you. Jesus said, *"You have heard that it was said, 'Love your neighbor and hate your enemy.' But I tell you: Love your enemies..."(Matthew 5:43).*

Pray for your enemies. Jesus said: *"...pray for those who persecute you, that you may be sons of your Father in heaven" (Matthew 5:44-45).* You are to pray blessings over those who persecute you (Romans 12:14).

Know that nothing can separate you from God's love--not even persecution or death (Romans 8:35-39).

Keep your focus on eternity. If you suffer with Him and in His behalf, you will be glorified with Him (Romans 8:16-18)

Know that God's grace is sufficient. No matter what you suffer, His grace is sufficient (2 Corinthians 12:9-10). You will have sufficient grace to help you in times of need (Hebrews 4:16).

Do not back down. If you are suffering because of your Christian witness, do not back down. The disciples suffered in this way, but they determined to continue to minister the Gospel and to obey God rather than man (Acts 4:18-20; 5:28-29).

WHAT GOD'S WORD SAYS ABOUT PERSECUTION:

O Lord my God, I take refuge in you; save and deliver me from all who pursue me. (Psalm 7:1)

Blessed are those who are persecuted because of righteousness, for theirs is the kingdom of heaven. Blessed are you when people insult you, persecute you and falsely say all kinds of evil against you because of me. Rejoice and be glad, because great is your reward in heaven, for in the same way they persecuted the prophets who were before you. (Matthew 5:10-12)

You have heard that it was said, 'Love your neighbor and hate your enemy.' But I tell you: Love your enemies and pray for those who persecute you, that you may be sons of your Father in heaven. (Matthew 5:43-45)

Forgive us our debts, as we also have forgiven our debtors. (Matthew 6:12)

But before all this, they will lay hands on you and persecute you. They will deliver you to synagogues and prisons, and you will be brought before kings and governors, and all on account of my name. This will result in your being witnesses to them. But make up your mind not to worry beforehand how you will defend yourselves. For I will give you words and wisdom that none of your adversaries will be able to resist or contradict. You will be betrayed even by parents, brothers, relatives and friends, and they will put some of you to death. All men will hate you because of me. But not a hair of your head will perish. By standing firm, you will gain life. (Luke 21:12-19)

If the world hates you, keep in mind that it hated me first. If you belonged to the world, it would love you as its own. As it is, you do not belong to the world, but I have chosen you out of the world. That is why the world hates you. Remember the words I spoke to you: 'No servant is greater than his master.' If they persecuted me, they will persecute you also. If they obeyed my teaching, they will obey yours also. They will treat you this way because of my name, for they do not know the One who sent me (John 15:18-21)

All this I have told you so that you will not go astray. They will put you out of the synagogue; in fact, a time is coming when anyone who kills you will think he is offering a service to God. They will do such things because they have not known the Father or me. I have told you this, so that when the time comes you will remember that I warned you. I did not tell you this at first because I was with you. (John 16:1-4)

I have given them your word and the world has hated them, for they are not of the world any more than I am of the world. My prayer is not that you take them out of the world but that you protect them from the evil one. They are not of the world, even as I am not of it. (John 17:14-16)

Then they called them in again and commanded them not to speak or teach at all in the name of Jesus. But Peter and John replied, "Judge for yourselves whether it is right in God's sight to obey you rather than God. For we cannot help speaking about what we have seen and heard." (Acts 4:18-20)

"We gave you strict orders not to teach in this name," he said. "Yet you have filled Jerusalem with your teaching and are determined to make us guilty of this man's blood." Peter and the other apostles replied: "We must obey God rather than men!" (Acts 5:28-29)

They preached the good news in that city and won a large number of disciples. Then they returned to Lystra, Iconium and Antioch, strengthening the disciples and encouraging them to remain true to the faith. "We must go through many hardships to enter the kingdom of God," they said. (Acts 14:21-22)

For I consider that the sufferings of this present time are not worthy to be compared with the glory which shall be revealed in us. (Romans 8:18)

Who shall separate us from the love of Christ? Shall tribulation, or distress, or persecution, or famine, or nakedness, or peril, or sword? As it is written: "For Your sake we are killed all day long; We are accounted as sheep for the slaughter." Yet in all these things we are more than conquerors through Him who loved us. For I am persuaded that neither death nor life, nor angels nor principalities nor powers, nor things present nor things to come, nor height nor depth, nor any other created thing, shall be able to separate us from the love of God which is in Christ Jesus our Lord. (Romans 8:35-39)

Bless those who persecute you; bless and do not curse. (Romans 12:14)

We are hard pressed on every side, but not crushed; perplexed, but not in despair; persecuted, but not abandoned; struck down, but not destroyed. (2 Corinthians 4:8-9)

But he said to me, "My grace is sufficient for you, for my power is made perfect in weakness." Therefore, I will boast all the more gladly about my weaknesses, so that Christ's power may rest on me. That is why, for Christ's sake, I delight in weaknesses, in insults, in hardships, in persecutions, in difficulties. For when I am weak, then I am strong. (2 Corinthians 12:9-10)

And pray that we may be delivered from wicked and evil men, for not everyone has faith. (2 Thessalonians 3:1-2)

In fact, everyone who wants to live a godly life in Christ Jesus will be persecuted. (2 Timothy 3:12)

Let us then approach the throne of grace with confidence, so that we may receive mercy and find grace to help us in our time of need. (Hebrews 4:16)

By faith Moses, when he had grown up, refused to be known as the son of Pharaoh's daughter. He chose to be mistreated along with the people of God rather than to enjoy the pleasures of sin for a short time. He regarded disgrace for the sake of Christ as of greater value than the treasures of Egypt, because he was looking ahead to his reward. (Hebrews 11:24-26)

Dear friends, do not be surprised at the painful trial you are suffering, as though something strange were happening to you. But rejoice that you participate in the sufferings of Christ, so that you may be overjoyed when his glory is revealed. If you are insulted because of the name of Christ, you are blessed, for the Spirit of glory and of God rests on you. If you suffer, it should not be as a murderer or thief or any other kind of criminal, or even as a meddler. However, if you suffer as a Christian, do not be ashamed, but praise God that you bear that name. (1 Peter 4:12-16)

CHAPTER ELEVEN

The "it" of Hypocrisy

DEFINITION: Hypocrisy is the claim or pretense of holding standards, beliefs, qualities opinions, virtues, and behaviors that one does not actual possess. In a biblical sense, a hypocrite confesses and claims salvation and spiritual maturity when they are actually void of these qualities. Some versions of the Bible translate "hypocrite" as "godless person." A hypocrite is one who acts a false part, makes a false profession, and is a deceiver, imposter, and cheater.

FACTS ABOUT HYPOCRISY:

Hypocrisy is instigated by Satan. The Word describes Satan as a "liar," and that is exactly what hypocrites do: They lie and deceive. 1 Timothy 4:2 speaks of "deceiving spirits", and that is what operates in the lives of hypocrites.

Hypocrisy is sinful.   Because lies and deceit are condemned by God, they are sinful.

There are hypocrites in every realm of life. Just as you would not judge all businessmen by one dishonest businessman, do not judge true believers by what you see in the life of a hypocrite.

Jesus taught against hypocrisy. He condemned the Pharisees, who were the religious leaders of the day, for their hypocrisy. See Matthew 6:2-6 and Matthew 23:13-32.

Hypocrites are legalists. First Timothy 4:3 states that hypocrites forbid people to marry and order them to abstain from certain foods. They demand of others what they, themselves, do not adhere to (Matthew 23:2-3).

Hypocrites are critical. Jesus described them as being concerned over a "speck of sawdust" in the eyes of others, while ignoring the "plank" in their own eyes (Matthew 7:3-5).

Their worship is in vain. Jesus said that hypocrites honor Him with their speech, but their hearts are far from Him, so their worship is in vain (Matthew 15:7-9).

Hypocrites look good on the outside. By outward appearances, you might think they are true believers, but they are not (Luke 11:39-44).

Hypocrites teach demonic doctrines. According to 1 Timothy 4:3, deceiving spirits and things taught by demon's cause people to abandon the faith.

DEALING WITH HYPOCRISY:

Ask God to forgive you if you have been living a hypocritical life. Hypocrisy is sin, and as all sin, must be confessed and forgiven.

Study the Word of God. The Word is truth and will help you live in truth rather than by deceitful doctrines that foster hypocrisy.

Separate yourself from hypocrites. Do not make hypocrites your close friends because you become like those with whom you associate (Proverbs 22:24).

Do not sit under the teaching of hypocrites. If the life-style of your minister, teacher, or spiritual leader does not line up with their confession, do not continue to sit under their teaching. It is deceptive and will cause you to depart from the faith (1 Timothy 4:1-2).

WHAT GOD'S WORD SAYS ABOUT HYPOCRISY:

For what is the hope of the hypocrite, though he may gain much, if God takes away his life? (Job 27:8, NKJV)

The hypocrite with his mouth destroys his neighbor, but through knowledge the righteous will be delivered. (Proverbs 11:9, NKJV)

So, when you give to the needy, do not announce it with trumpets, as the hypocrites do in the synagogues and on the streets, to be honored by men. I tell you the truth, they have received their reward in full. But when you give to the needy, do not let your left hand know what your right hand is doing, so that your giving may be in secret. Then your Father, who sees what is done in secret, will reward you. And when you pray, do not be like the hypocrites, for they love to pray standing in the synagogues and on the street corners to be seen by men. I tell you the truth, they have received their reward in full. But when you pray, go into your room, close the door and pray to your Father, who is unseen. Then your Father, who sees what is done in secret, will reward you. (Matthew 6:2-6)

Why do you look at the speck of sawdust in your brother's eye and pay no attention to the plank in your own eye? How can you say to your brother, 'Let me take the speck out of your eye,' when all the time there is a plank in your own eye? You hypocrite, first take the plank out of your own eye, and then you will see clearly to remove the speck from your brother's eye. (Matthew 7:3-5)

You hypocrites! Isaiah was right when he prophesied about you: "'These people honor me with their lips, but their hearts are far from me. They worship me in vain; their teachings are but rules taught by men." (Matthew 15:7-9)

The teachers of the law and the Pharisees sit in Moses' seat. So, you must obey them and do everything they tell you. But do not do what they do, for they do not practice what they preach. (Matthew 23:2-3)

Woe to you, teachers of the law and Pharisees, you hypocrites! You shut the kingdom of heaven in men's faces. You yourselves do not enter, nor will you let those enter who are trying to. Woe to you, teachers of the law and Pharisees, you hypocrites! You travel over land and sea to win a single convert, and when he becomes one, you make him twice as much a son of hell as you are. Woe to you, blind guides! You say, 'If anyone swears by the temple, it means nothing; but if anyone swears by the gold of the temple, he is bound by his oath.' You blind fools! Which is greater: the gold, or the temple that makes the gold sacred? You also say, 'If anyone swears by the altar, it means nothing; but if anyone swears by the gift on it, he is bound by his oath.' You blind men! Which is greater: the gift, or the altar that makes the gift sacred? Therefore, he who swears by the altar swears by it and by everything on it. And he who swears by the temple swears by it and by the one who dwells in it. And he who swears by heaven swears by God's throne and by the one who sits on it. Woe to you, teachers of the law and Pharisees, you hypocrites! You give a tenth of your spices--mint, dill and cumin. But you have neglected the more important matters of the law--justice, mercy and faithfulness. You should have practiced the latter, without neglecting the former. You blind guides! You strain out a gnat but swallow a camel. Woe to you, teachers of the law and Pharisees, you hypocrites! You clean the outside of the cup and dish, but inside they are full of greed and self-indulgence. Blind Pharisee! First clean the inside of the cup and dish, and then the outside also will be clean. Woe to you, teachers of the law and Pharisees, you hypocrites! You are like whitewashed tombs, which look beautiful on the outside but on the inside, are full of dead men's bones and everything unclean. In the same way, on the outside you appear to people as righteous but on the inside, you are full of hypocrisy and wickedness. Woe to you, teachers of the law and Pharisees, you hypocrites! You build tombs for the prophets and decorate the graves of the righteous. And you say, 'If we had lived in the days of our forefathers, we would not have taken part with them in shedding the blood of the prophets.' So, you testify against yourselves that you are the descendants of those who murdered the prophets. Fill up, then, the measure of the sin of your forefathers! You snakes! You brood of vipers! How will you escape being condemned to hell? (Matthew 23:13-32)

These people honor me with their lips, but their hearts are far from me. They worship me in vain; their teachings are but rules taught by men. You have let go of the commands of God and are holding on to the traditions of men. (Mark 7:6-8)

Then the Lord said to him, "Now then, you Pharisees clean the outside of the cup and dish, but inside you are full of greed and wickedness. You foolish people! Did not the one who made the outside make the inside also? But give what is inside [the dish] to the poor, and everything will be clean for you. Woe to you Pharisees, because you give God a tenth of your mint, rue and all other kinds of garden herbs, but you neglect justice and the love of God. You should have practiced the latter without leaving the former undone. Woe to you Pharisees, because you love the most important seats in the synagogues and greetings in the marketplaces. Woe to you, because you are like unmarked graves, which men walk over without knowing it." (Luke 11:39-44)

Hypocrites! You know how to interpret the appearance of the earth and the sky. How is it that you don't know how to interpret this present time? (Luke 12:56)

Beware of the teachers of the law. They like to walk around in flowing robes and love to be greeted in the marketplaces and have the most important seats in the synagogues and the places of honor at banquets. They devour widows' houses and for a show make lengthy prayers. Such men will be punished most severely. (Luke 20:46-47)

The Spirit clearly says that in later times some will abandon the faith and follow deceiving spirits and things taught by demons. Such teachings come through hypocritical liars, whose consciences have been seared as with a hot iron. (1 Timothy 4:1-2)

CHAPTER TWELVE

The "it" of Lack of Peace

DEFINITION: Peace is a condition of quiet, calm, tranquility, and harmony. It is the absence of strife, anxiety, and concern. Peace is not just passivity, because maintaining peace requires directed action on the part of a peacemaker. In Greek, "peace" means to bind together in wholeness.

FACTS ABOUT PEACE:

There are two types of peace. The first is peace *with* God which comes through accepting Christ as Savior (Romans 5:1). After you have made peace with God, you can have the peace *of* God manifested in your life (Philippians 4:7).

You must know God to experience true peace. You will never experience true peace apart from making peace with God. You do this by confessing and repenting of sin and--if you are not a believer--accepting Jesus Christ as Savior. Jesus is the Prince of Peace, enabling you to have both peace with God and the peace of God (Ephesians 2:14).

Lack of peace results from wrong attitudes and sinful actions. Worries over provision--a job, housing, clothes, food, money to pay bills--often result in a lack of peace. Jesus said not to concern yourself with these things (Matthew 6:31-34). Unconfessed sin will also cause you to lose your peace.

Lack of peace can be caused by tormenting spirits. Demonic spirits bring tormenting thoughts that steal your peace.

Peace is a gift from God. It is a spiritual legacy bestowed by Jesus: *"Peace I leave with you; my peace I give you. I do not give to you as the world gives. Do not let your hearts be troubled and do not be afraid" (John 14:27).*

Peace is a Fruit of the Holy Spirit. As one of the Fruit of the Spirit, it is a virtue that is to be developed in the lives of all believers (Galatians 5:22).

Peace is a benefit of the atonement of Christ. The Prophet Isaiah declared: *"But he was pierced for our transgressions, he was crushed for our iniquities; the punishment that brought us peace was upon him, and by his wounds we are healed" (Isaiah 53:5).*

Confusion is the opposite of peace. God is not the author of confusion, rather He is the God of peace (1 Corinthians 14:33).

DEALING WITH PEACE:

Make peace with God. If you do not know Jesus as Savior or there is known sin in your life, make peace with God.   Confess, repent, and ask forgiveness. There is no peace without the Prince of Peace. You must have peace with God in order to experience the peace of God.

Bind tormenting spirits. Bind the spirits that bring confusion and the tormenting thoughts that cause you to lose your peace. Loose the spirit of peace to operate in your life.

Accept peace as a gift from God. Just as you accepted salvation, accept peace as God's gift to you (John 14:27) and a Fruit of the Holy Spirit (Galatians 5:22).

Ask God to transform your mind. Lack of peace begins with your thought life..."*Therefore, I urge you, brothers, in view of God's mercy, to offer your bodies as living sacrifices, holy and pleasing to God--this is your spiritual act of worship. Do not conform any longer to the pattern of this world, but be transformed by the renewing of your mind. Then you will be able to test and approve what God's will is--his good, pleasing and perfect will" (Romans 12:1-2).*

Keep your mind focused on God. Despite adversities and the circumstances of life, keep your mind focused on God (Isaiah 26:3). You can do this through continual prayer and study of the Word, for one of the purposes of the Word is to bring peace (John 16:33).

Allow peace to reign. You must allow or "let" the peace of God to reign in your life despite the circumstances: *"Let the peace of Christ rule in your hearts, since as members of one body you were called to peace" (Colossians 3:15).*

WHAT GOD'S WORD SAYS ABOUT PEACE:

I will both lie down in peace, and sleep; For You alone, O Lord, make me dwell in safety. (Psalm 4:8)

The Lord gives strength to his people; the Lord blesses his people with peace. (Psalm 29:11)

Turn from evil and do good; seek peace and pursue it. (Psalm 34:14)

Consider the blameless, observe the upright; there is a future for the man of peace. (Psalm 37:37)

When you lie down, you will not be afraid; when you lie down, your sleep will be sweet. (Proverbs 3:24)

When a man's ways are pleasing to the Lord, he makes even his enemies live at peace with him. (Proverbs 16:7)

The beginning of strife is like releasing water; Therefore, stop contention before a quarrel starts. (Proverbs 17:14, NKJV)

For to us a child is born, to us a son is given, and the government will be on his shoulders.

And he will be called Wonderful Counselor, Mighty God, Everlasting Father, Prince of Peace. Of the increase of his government and peace there will be no end. (Isaiah 9:6-7)

You will keep in perfect peace him whose mind is steadfast, because he trusts in you. (Isaiah 26:3)

The fruit of righteousness will be peace; the effect of righteousness will be quietness and confidence forever. (Isaiah 32:17)

So, do not fear, for I am with you; do not be dismayed, for I am your God. I will strengthen you and help you; I will uphold you with my righteous right hand. (Isaiah 41:10)

If only you had paid attention to my commands, your peace would have been like a river, your righteousness like the waves of the sea. (Isaiah 48:18)

"There is no peace," says the Lord, "for the wicked." (Isaiah 48:22)

But he was pierced for our transgressions, he was crushed for our iniquities; the punishment that brought us peace was upon him, and by his wounds we are healed. (Isaiah 53:5)

"Though the mountains be shaken and the hills be removed, yet my unfailing love for you will not be shaken nor my covenant of peace be removed," says the Lord, who has compassion on you. (Isaiah 54:10)

All your sons will be taught by the Lord, and great will be your children's peace. (Isaiah 54:13)

You will go out in joy and be led forth in peace; the mountains and hills will burst into song before you, and all the trees of the field will clap their hands. (Isaiah 55:12)

"I know the plans I have for you," declares the Lord, "plans to prosper you and not to harm you, plan to give you hope and a future." (Jeremiah 29:11)

Blessed are the peacemakers, for they will be called sons of God. (Matthew 5:9)

Salt is good, but if the salt loses its flavor, how will you season it? Have salt in yourselves, and have peace with one another. (Mark 9:50, NKJV)

Peace I leave with you; my peace I give you. I do not give to you as the world gives. Do not let your hearts be troubled and do not be afraid. (John 14:27)

I have told you these things, so that in me you may have peace. In this world you will have trouble. But take heart! I have overcome the world. (John 16:33)

The mind of sinful man is death, but the mind controlled by the Spirit is life and peace; (Romans 8:6)

Therefore, I urge you, brothers, in view of God's mercy, to offer your bodies as living sacrifices, holy and pleasing to God--this is your spiritual act of worship. Do not conform any longer to the pattern of this world, but be transformed by the renewing of your mind. Then you will be able to test and approve what God's will is--his good, pleasing and perfect will. (Romans 12:1-2)

If possible, so far as it depends on you, be at peace with all men. (Romans 12:18)

For the kingdom of God is not meat and drink; but righteousness, and peace, and joy in the Holy Ghost. (Romans 14:17)

Let us therefore follow after the things which make for peace, and things wherewith one may edify another. (Romans 14:19, KJV)

Now the God of hope fill you with all joy and peace in believing, that ye may abound in hope, through the power of the Holy Ghost. (Romans 15:13)

For God is not a God of disorder but of peace. (1 Corinthians 14:33)

...Aim for perfection, listen to my appeal, be of one mind, live in peace. And the God of love and peace will be with you. (2 Corinthians 13:11)

But the fruit of the Spirit is love, joy, peace, patience, kindness, goodness, faithfulness, gentleness and self-control. Against such things there is no law. (Galatians 5:22-23)

For he himself is our peace, who has made the two one and has destroyed the barrier, the dividing wall of hostility, by abolishing in his flesh the law with its commandments and regulations. His purpose was to create in himself one new man out of the two, thus making peace, and in this one body to reconcile both of them to God through the cross, by which he put to death their hostility. He came and preached peace to you who were far away and peace to those who were near. For through him we both have access to the Father by one Spirit. (Ephesians 2:14-18)

Make every effort to keep the unity of the Spirit through the bond of peace. (Ephesians 4:3)

Be anxious for nothing, but in everything by prayer and supplication, with thanksgiving, let your requests be made known to God; and the peace of God, which surpasses all understanding, will guard your hearts and minds through Christ Jesus. (Philippians 4:6-7, NKJV)

For God was pleased to have all his fullness dwell in him, and through him to reconcile to himself all things, whether things on earth or things in heaven, by making peace through his blood, shed on the cross. (Colossians 1:19-20)

Let the peace of Christ rule in your hearts, since as members of one body you were called to peace. (Colossians 3:15).

Now may the Lord of peace Himself give you peace always in every way. The Lord be with you all. (2 Thessalonians 3:16, NKJV)

Make every effort to live in peace with all men and to be holy; without holiness no one will see the Lord. (Hebrews 12:14)

But the wisdom that is from above is first pure, then peaceable, gentle, easy to be entreated, full of mercy and good fruits, without variance, without hypocrisy. And the fruit of righteousness is sown in peace for them that make peace. (James 3:17-18, ASV)

Let him turn away from evil and do good; Let him seek peace and pursue it. (1 Peter 3:11, NKJV)

Cast all your anxiety on him because he cares for you. (1 Peter 5:7)

CONCLUSION

How to Get Rid of "it" though Personal Deliverance

When you understand self-deliverance, you will keep yourself from being bond; you will keep yourself healthy, physically and spiritually and be free from spiritual pollution. Every day, you will enjoy divine health and will not be spending your money on drugs and hospital bills.

Sometimes, there may not be a minister who is anointed and knowledgeable about deliverance to help you. Sometimes, you can be heavily attacked and the next service is about four days away. What do you do? You should never allow evil spirits to reside in your life. If you lack adequate time to do a self-deliverance in the mornings, after your quiet time, then, when you're having your bath, you could do it.

Whatever the causes of our spiritual afflictions, there are several proven steps we may try to help ourselves find freedom and healing. If these steps do not resolve your situation, then perhaps it is time to ask for help:

Step 1 — Conversion

Deliverance from any level of bondage, or harassment (collectively called, "spiritual afflictions") cannot be achieved without personal conversion. Deliverance from milder forms of spiritual affliction may often be achieved by the various acts of personal conversion—Acts of Contrition, Faith, Hope, Charity, and Consecration. "Prayer Acts" and other prayers, with fasting, and various devotions are often effective to drive evil spirits away:

So humble yourselves before God. Resist the Devil, and he will flee from you. Draw close to God, and God will draw close to you. — (James 4:7,8)

The first step, therefore, is make up your mind to live the Christ-life; or if already doing so, to persevere in living the Christ-life. This internal conversion, which is a conscious decision and determination to follow Christ and all of His teachings, precedes all other steps to deliverance. Without conversion to the Faith in Jesus Christ and participation in His family, the Church, deliverance, even if seemingly effective for a while, cannot be successful in the long run. It is the *"Truth"* that makes us free (John 8:31b), not prayers, rituals, counseling, or personal will in themselves. It is the confrontation with Truth that sends the demons running back to hell. This is why the method of Deliverance Counseling we use is called a *"Truth Encounter"*. As demons are confronted with the Truth, and as we are confronted with the Truth, of whom we are in Christ, we gain freedom. The foundation of all truth is Jesus Christ, who is Truth (John 14:6). Without our Lord Jesus Christ, we can never know truth or obtain it.

Some people believe they are unable to make a profession of faith in Jesus Christ. In such cases the person should ask God for help—ask Him for the faith that will save, deliver, and heal.

If we are willing to accept the gift of faith from God, our Lord will give it to us when we ask:

And I tell you, Ask, and it will be given you; seek, and you will find; knock, and it will be opened to you. For every one who asks receives, and he who seeks finds, and to him who knocks it will be opened. What father among you, if his son asks for a fish, will instead of a fish give him a serpent; or if he asks for an egg, will give him a scorpion? If you then, who are evil, know how to give good gifts to your children, how much more will the heavenly Father give the Holy Spirit to those who ask him! — (Luke 11:9-13)

Sincerely ask God for the faith that brings saving faith, the faith of conversion to the One, that is Jesus Christ, whom who declares:

I am the way, and the truth, and the life; no one comes to the Father, but by me (John 14:6) .... Come to me, all who labor and are heavy laden, and I will give you rest (Matthew 11:28) .... I will not reject anyone who comes to me (John 6:37) .... [rather] take my yoke upon you, and learn from me; for I am gentle and lowly in heart, and you will find rest for your souls. For my yoke is easy, and my burden is light (Matt 11:29-30)

Step 2 — Repentance

Essential to growing closer to God in faith, devotion, and love is to repent of those behaviors, desires, beliefs, and ideas that are sinful. The definition of sin is much broader than most people imagine. A definition of sin:

Sin is an offense against reason, truth, and right conscience; it is a failure in genuine love for God and neighbor caused by a perverse attachment to certain goods. Its wounds the nature of man and injures human solidarity. It has been defined as "an utterance, a deed, or a desire contrary to the eternal law."

Sin is an offense against God: *"Against you, you alone, have I sinned, and done that which is evil in your sight"* (Ps 51:4). Sin sets itself against God's love for us and turns our hearts away from it. Like the first sin (of Adam and Eve), it is disobedience, a revolt against God through the will to become "like gods" (Gen 3:5), knowing and determining good and evil. Sin is thus "love of oneself even to contempt of God." In this proud self-exaltation, sin is diametrically opposed to the obedience of Jesus, which achieves our salvation (cf. Phil 2:6-9).

We must repent of our sin, but repentance involves more than merely "turning away" from sin. Repentance must also renounce all that opposes God and all that He finds sinful. This includes renouncing Satan and his ways, renouncing personal sins, and renouncing all that leads us to sin. Some of the common sins and situations that interfere with deliverance include: involvement in non-Christian activities like the occult; persistent situational sins such as living together without marriage or remarriage without annulment of previous marriages; maintaining improper or problematic friendships; illegal activities of any sort; and sins that have become habitual such as pornography, masturbation, fornication, gossip, lying, stealing, etc.

The three greatest stumbling blocks to deliverance is Pride, Rebellion, and Unforgiveness and all the things that go along with those three sins. Repentance of Pride, Rebellion, and Unforgiveness is required to even hope for deliverance. Repentance also includes the firm amendment to avoid sin, and the near occasion of sin, in the future. Repentance requires a *complete* turnaround of our lives, a becoming a *"new man"*, so that...

...you should put away the old self of your former way of life, corrupted through deceitful desires, and be renewed in the spirit of your minds, and put on the new self, created in God's way in righteousness and holiness of truth. Therefore, putting away falsehood, speak the truth, each one to his neighbor, for we are members one of another...(thus) do not leave room for the devil (Eph 4:22-25,26b)

Step 3 — Confession

With faith and contrition of heart, repentance of mind, firm purpose to avoid sin and that which leads us to sin, we must now confess our sins before our God who is a God of forgiveness and mercy. This is a critical step that we will discuss at length.

The manner of our confession differs, but within our respective traditions, confession is required:

If we confess our sins, he is faithful and just, and will forgive our sins and cleanse us from all unrighteousness. (1 John 1:9)

... if you confess with your mouth that Jesus is Lord and believe in your heart that God raised him from the dead, you will be saved. For one believes with the heart and so is justified, and one confesses with the mouth and so is saved. (Romans 10:9-10)

"Confess your sins to each other and pray for each other so that you may be healed. The earnest prayer of a righteous person has great power and wonderful results" (James 5:16).

This confidant maybe one's pastor or another minister, or a trusted friend. We must be careful when choosing an "accountability partner." Since we will be revealing very private and sensitive information about ourselves, it is critically important to trust whoever we choose as a confidant to be discreet and to keep absolutely confidential the information we tell them.

There is wisdom in presenting oneself to an "accountability partner." Personal accountability is upheld when we confess to another person whom may hold us accountable for our actions. Confessing our sins to one another is a powerful way to break the bonds of sin in our lives. It is much harder to confess our sins to one another than to simply say, *"Lord, forgive me"*. While God is forgiving, of course, it is the demands of personal accountability before another human being that brings our confession into grounded reality that strengthens our commitment to turn away from sin in the future.

Religious ministers, psychologists, counselors, and others including the Deliverance Counselors of agency, are also bound either by law, ethical codes, or contract with the client (or bound by any combination thereof) to keep private and confidential all that is revealed to them. In addition, those in the ministerial and helping professions are usually trained in the ethics, legalities, and culture of maintaining confidentiality. They are use to keeping private the personal information of their patients and clients. Friends, on the other hand, may not have such training and may not be use to the culture of confidentiality. Thus, if one's confidant is not a pastor, or at least a minister, psychologist, or counselor bound by law and/or ethical codes, take care to ensure the chosen confidant understands thoroughly that he must keep private all that he hears and may not discuss it with anyone, not even with his spouse.

There is a great psychological comfort in hearing the words, "I forgive you" or the equivalent, "I absolve you of your sins." Our Father in heaven understands this psychological need. Thus, in His great love for us, He provided a way for us to hear those words in His name. It is God who ultimately forgives sins, but God, according to His sovereign authority chose to delegate this authority to His validly ordained priests. This power was given to the Apostles in John 20:22-23 and was passed on from them to those whom they appointed.

Our Father in heaven also knows and understands our need to be a family and for the family to come to our aid when we are hurting, to offer forgiveness when we fall, and to provide healing and strength to help us grow in faith. God forgives you when you appeal to Him with your heart-felt and sincere repentance and confession. Follow the tradition of your denomination and always offer a prayer for forgiveness as soon as possible after sinning. Then, in obedience to the Bible, seek accountability by confession to a confidant to complete your healing.

Step 4 — Removing the Greatest Stumbling blocks: Pride, Rebellion, and Forgiveness

We have already mentioned that the three biggest stumbling blocks to deliverance is usually Pride, Rebellion, and Unforgiveness. These three sins distance us from God. To draw closer to God we need to give up our pride, obey our Lord's teachings, and forgive those who hurt us.

In Deliverance Counseling we help our clients through exercises to locate pockets of pride and rebellion and to rid themselves of these sins with the help of God through prayer. Forgiveness, however, tends to be the most difficult, partly because of pride or even rebellion perhaps, but mostly because of deeply emotional issues surrounding the circumstances of the hurts someone has given us. Whatever the causes of our unforgiveness, deliverance is not possible until we can come to forgive, thus we shall discuss this topic at some length too.

The following guide is rather long, but this step is one of the most important. One simple MUST deals with Pride, Rebellion, and Unforgiveness if deliverance and healing is to be permanently possible.

Pride: Pride is the essential sin that leads to most other sins. It is the sin of Lucifer that led him to rebel against God resulting in his expulsion from heaven and becoming Satan.

Pride is a killer. Pride says, "I can do it! I can get myself out of this mess without God and without anyone else's helped." No, we can't! We absolutely need God, and we desperately need each other.

Pride also says "I know the best and most efficient way and how dare others get in the way of that" or "How dare things not go my way" or "How dare some person or something get in the way of what I want to do." Impatience is a factor of pride. Other ways impatience reveals our pride is getting impatient when we cannot find our car keys, or when we are late to a meeting, or if someone is driving too slowly for us on the hi-way, or when the computer acts up and interrupts our train of thought.

Impatience is the sister to Pride because it is caused essentially by our desire to have things our own way, in our own time, and according to our own preferences.

Pride is also the engine behind egotism (thinking more of oneself than one ought) and behind false humility (putting oneself down to be less than what one actually is). Pride is the force behind resistance to lawful and appropriate authority — whether that authority is a parent, teacher, police officer, government, employer, or the Church.

Pride is the basis of thinking of oneself as better than others, being pompous, and having contempt toward one's neighbors, employers, other family members, or the Church and her ministers.

Pride can also rear its ugly head in more subtle ways such as reluctance to apologize when we need to apologize, demanding our rights merely because it is our right, being inappropriately unkind or rude, jealousy, being quick-tempered, moodiness, brooding over wrongs done by others to oneself, depression and despair, or demanding that we are right about something, when indeed we are right about the issue, even though the issue is unimportant or can be handled differently (this is a major phenomenon in marriages, families, and friendships — the phrase "We need to choose our battles" is an important remedy for this).

Other ways that Pride expresses itself include: by taking personal credit for gifts or possessions and thus refusing to acknowledge that we have what we have by God's Providence; glorying in our achievements as if they were not primary a result of God's grace and divine goodness; by minimizing one's defeats; by claiming qualities that are not actually possessed; magnifying the faults and defects of others or dwelling upon the defects and faults of others.

James 4:6-10 and 1 Peter 5:1-10 reveals that spiritual conflict follows pride.

Examine yourself for these and any other attributes of pride and then pray:

Dear Heavenly Father. You have said that pride goes before destruction and an arrogant spirit before stumbling (Prov. 16:18). I confess that I have not denied myself, picked up my cross daily, and followed You (Matt. 16:24). In so doing I have given ground to the enemy in my life. I have believed that I could be successful and live victoriously by my own strength and resources. I now confess that I have sinned against You by placing my will before You and by centering my life around self instead of You.

I now renounce the self-life and by so doing cancel all the ground that has been gained in my life by the enemies of the Lord Jesus Christ. I pray that You will guide me so that I will do nothing from selfishness or empty conceit, but with humility of mind that I will regard others as more important than myself (Phil. 2:3). Enable me through love to serve others and in honor prefer others (Rom. 12:10). Amen.

Rebellion: We often place our confidence in the flesh not only with the "I can do it myself" attitude but each time we assert our own opinions above the teachings of Christ. It is a pride and a rebellion to say, "I want to do it my way" or "I want to think the way I want" without regard to the ways God teaches us to go and to believe. This is an arrogance that not only can get us into major trouble but also forms a major vulnerability for demons to come into our life.

Rebelling against God and His authority gives Satan an opportunity to attack. As our commanding general, the Lord Jesus Christ says, *"Get into ranks and follow Me. I will not lead you into temptation, but I will deliver you from evil."*

The Bible teaches us that it is the will of God for us to be obedient to parents, to civil government, to the Church, and to the pastors who are over us. We have two biblical responsibilities in regard to these authority figures: 1) Pray for them; and 2) submit to them. The only time God permits us to disobey those in authority over us is when they require of us an act or acquiescence in ways that are contrary to Church Law, Natural Law, or Divine Law.

Being under authority is an act of faith; we are trusting God to work through His established lines of authority. The authority that God has ordained does not mean, however, that we are to submit to abuse from those authorities. In those cases where someone in authority over us is abusing us in any way, then we need to act in appropriate ways according to the situation — such as appeal to the state for protection and relief for civil or criminal issues; or appeal to Church authorities on some issue involving religion or our parish; or make appropriate decisions such as terminating an abusive relationship, etc. Whoever the authority, who is abusing, we need to pray for the offender and to forgive him; but we are not required to be a doormat or target of their abuse.

Some of the lines of authority mentioned in the Bible include:

- Church leaders (Hebrews 13:17; Matthew 18:15-18)
- Parents (Ephesians 6: 1-3; Exodus 20:12)
- Husbands (1 Peter 3:1-3; Ephesians 5:23-24)
- Employers (1 Peter 2:18-21)
- Civil Government (Romans 13:1-5; 1 Timothy 2:1-3; 1 Peter 2:13-16)

Examine yourself for any areas of rebellion (deliberate driving faster than the speed limit is rebellion, too, you know!) and then pray:

Dear Heavenly Father. You have said that rebellion is as the sin of witchcraft and insubordination is as iniquity and idolatry (1 Sam. 15.23). I know that in action and attitude I have sinned against You with a rebellious heart. I ask Your forgiveness for my rebellion and pray that by the shed blood of the Lord Jesus Christ, strengthened by intercession of the that all ground gained by evil spirits because of my rebelliousness be canceled and taken back. I pray that You will shed light on all my ways that I may know the full extent of my rebelliousness, and I now choose to adopt a submissive spirit and a servant's heart. Amen.

Unforgiveness: Jesus Himself discusses the seriousness of failing to forgive. He tells us that failure to forgive those who hurt us will result in our not being forgiven ourselves by God. *"Forgive us our trespasses (sins) as we forgive those who trespass (sin) against us"*. The *Our Father*, the Lord's Prayer, which most all of us know and pray, Jesus teaches us that God will be as forgiving to us as we are to others.

Indeed, how can we expect God to forgive us when we do not forgive our brothers? Consider the follow teachings from Holy Scripture:

If you forgive those who sin against you, your heavenly Father will forgive you. But if you refuse to forgive others, your Father will not forgive your sins (Matthew 6:14,15).

But when you are praying, first forgive anyone you are holding a grudge against, so that your Father in heaven will forgive your sins, too (Mark 11:25).

If you forgive others, you will be forgiven. (Luke 6:37b)

Forgiveness is not about emotions and feelings. You can still be hurting, angry and upset and still decide to forgive. Forgiveness involves a mental decision, a decision of will, an act of your free will, even though you may not "Feel it".

The true nature of forgiveness:

1. **Forgiveness is not forgetting:** People who try to forget find that cannot. It is an unfortunate quirk of the English language with the phrase, "Forgive and forget". In actuality this phrase does not mean to "forget" in the sense of not remembering what happened; of course, we will remember. God says He will "remember our sins no more" (Heb. 10: 17), but God, being omniscient, obviously cannot literally forget. "Remember no more" means that God will never use the past against us (Ps. 103:12).

   To forget is really "to let go". We need to *"let go and let God"*. We let go of the past, but more importantly we let go of the hurt. As long as we do not forgive, as long as we do not let go, we allow the offender of our wounds continue to hurt us.
2. **Forgiveness is a choice not a feeling:** Since God requires us to forgive, <u>it is something we can do</u>. God will NEVER ask us to do something that is impossible for us to do; that would be cruel and God is a loving God.

   Forgiveness, however, is difficult for us because it pulls against our feelings and emotional hurts. Forgiveness is not about forgetting our feelings or our emotional hurts. We often will not "feel" like forgiving, but we must forgive anyway. As the Lord Prayer teaches us, God forgives us "as we forgive others". But how can God require this of us when we have been hurt so badly?

   God does not expect your feelings and emotional hurts to be healed overnight. He knows and understands our feelings and our hurts. He is a compassionate God and will help us to heal over time, as we are able. What God expects of us is not an immediate emotional healing, but a decision of will to forgive, a decision of will to trust Him to take care of the offender and to heal us, a decision of will to ask God for, and to commit to, being healed of our wounds.

3. **Forgiveness is not letting the person off the hook:** Forgiving is about you letting go, but it is not letting the offender off the hook. He will still pay for what he did, either before the Law or before God or both.

   Forgiving is surely difficult for us because it pulls against our concept of justice. We want revenge for offenses suffered. But we are told never to take our own revenge (Rom. 12:9). Revenge does more damage to us than it punishes the offender. God's justice will prevail, no one can escape it. Never fear, those who hurt us will be held accountable, but we must let God deal with it. In order for God to deal with it, we need to let Him deal with it by letting go.

   "Why should I let them off the hook?" But doing that is precisely the problem — we are still hooked to them, still bound by our past when we do not forgive.

   To forgive does not mean letting the person off the hook; it means letting yourself off the hook.

4. **But you don't understand how much this person hurt me:** The problem is that when we do not forgive we, in essence, allow the person to still hurt us! The question is, "How do we stop the pain?" The answer is **to forgive!**

   It is important to understand that we do not forgive someone for their sake; we do it for our sake so we can be free. Our need to forgive is not an issue between the offender and us; it is between us and God.

5. **Forgiveness is agreeing to live with the consequences of another's sin:** Forgiveness is costly. We pay the price of the evil we forgive. We are going to live with those consequences whether we want to or not; our only choice is whether or not we will do so in the slavery of bitterness and unforgiveness or with the freedom of forgiveness.

   Jesus took the consequences of our sin upon Himself. All true forgiveness is substitution because no one really forgives without bearing the consequences of the other person's sin. God the Father *"made Him who knew no sin to be sin on our behalf, that we might become the righteousness of God in Him"* (2 Cor. 5:2 1).

   Where is the justice? We might ask. It is the Cross that makes forgiveness legally and morally right: *"For the death that He died, He died to sin, once for all"* (Rom. 6: 10). This doesn't mean that we tolerate sin. We must always stand against sin, but we must give the offender to God and get on with our life.

6. **How do we forgive from our heart?** First, we acknowledge the hurt and the hate. If our forgiveness does not visit the emotional core of our life, it will be incomplete. Many feel the pain of interpersonal offenses, but they will not

acknowledge it. Let God bring the pain to the surface so He can deal with it. This is where the healing takes place.

Do not wait to forgive until we feel like forgiving; we will never get there. Feelings take time to heal mostly <u>after</u> the choice to forgive is made and Satan has lost his place (Eph. 4:26, 27). Freedom is what will be gained, not a feeling.

7. **Summary of Points on Forgiveness:**
    - Forgiveness is necessary to have fellowship with God.
    - It is not forgetting.
    - It is a choice.
    - Letting the offender off <u>our</u> hook is what frees us.
    - The offender is not off God's hook.
    - God says, "Revenge is mine."
    - You must acknowledge the hurt and the hate.
    - Forgiveness means we are agreeing to live with the consequences of another's sin — which we have to do anyway.
    - The justice is in the cross.
    - Choice is between the slavery of bitterness or the freedom of forgiveness.
    - Forgiveness means not using the past against the offender.
    - Forgiveness <u>does not</u> mean tolerating the sin or abuse.
    - Why forgive? To stop the pain! As we live in unforgiveness the offender still hurts us!
    - The issue of forgiveness is between you and God only.
    - The act of forgiveness is for your sake, and for your freedom.

Think about the people in your life for whom you need to forgive, people to whom you hold bitterness, people who have hurt you or disappointed you in anyway, or for whom you hold any kind of grudge. Be sure to ALWAYS include your parents, siblings, spouse, and YOURSELF. There is always something to forgive in our families and in ourselves.

Record all the names you can think of on a sheet of paper and a brief note as to why you need to forgive them. If you do not remember names, list them by what you do remember, such as "the guy in sixth grade with the red hat". If you cannot remember why you need to forgive someone on your list that is okay; forgive them for whatever it was — God knows.

After preparing this list ask God to bring to your mind anyone you have forgotten. It is not unusual to forget, or to push aside from our conscious mind, incidents and even the names of people whom have hurt us. These hidden hurts and wounds need to be healed as well. Thus, ask God to bring to your mind any person you have forgotten for whom you need to forgive, for whom you hold a grudge against, for which you are bitter, for those who have hurt you, with the following prayer:

Father in heaven, please bring to my mind the names of any people for whom I have held bitterness towards, grudges against, or have not forgiven for the hurts they have caused me. Help me to remember all these hurts so that they may be offered to You, O Lord, and healed from my soul so that I may live the truly victorious Christ-life. Amen.

Add to your list the names of anyone God may bring to your mind.

Now it is time to pray...

The following prayer needs to be said for each person on the list for which you need to forgive. Do not go to the next person on the list until you are sure you have dealt with all the remembered pain.

As you pray, God may bring to your mind various offending people and experiences that has been totally forgotten. Allow God to do this even if it is painful. Remember this process of forgiveness is for your sake because God wants you to be free.

Remember also that by forgiving the offender we are not rationalizing or trying to explain the offender's behavior. Forgiveness deals with the victim's pain, your pain, not another's excuses. Positive feelings will follow in time; freeing you from the past is the critical issue now.

If you are willing to forgive for your sake, so that you can walk away from this webpage free in Christ, free from the past and from person who hurt you, pray the introductory prayer below and then pray the "Prayer to Forgive" for each person on your list:

Heavenly Father, I now ask for your help in forgiving all those people on my list. Although I am still hurt and angry with them, I know that they are your children and that you love them more than I can possibly know. For this reason, my God, I ask you to help me forgive them. I lay down all bitterness, resentment and hatred for this person and I freely choose to forgive them. Teach me to be more merciful, my God, and help me be always willing, just as you are always willing, to forgive those who sin against me. Amen."

Prayer to Forgive

Lord, I forgive ________________________________ for (specifically identify all offenses and painful memories).

May God heal you and bless you!

Step 5 — Know Who You Are in Christ!

In order to gain freedom, it is important to know who you are in Christ. Thus, you need to evaluate the concept you have of yourself, to acknowledge the truth about God and about yourself; about your relationship and ideas about God and about the manner of our lives.

We often deceive ourselves about our position in Christ and our relationship with Him. For example, we may say to ourselves: "This isn't going to work" or "I wish I could believe this but I can't" or perhaps even more direct deceptions or denials concerning the promises of God for His children. Areas of deception that we may have include:

1. **Self-Deception** (telling ourselves things that are not true)

- o   Listening to God's words but thinking we do not have to do it (Ja 1:22; 4:17)
- o   Thinking we have no sin or do not sin (1 Jn 1:8)
- o   Thinking that we are something when we are not (Gal 6:3)
- o   Believing that we will not reap what we sow (Gal 6:7)
- o   Thinking we are wise and sophisticated in the 21st century (1 Cor 3:18, 19)
- o   Believing that the unrighteous will reach heaven (1 Cor 6:9)
- o   Thinking we can associate with bad company and not be corrupted (1 Cor 15:33)
2. **Self-Defense** (defending ourselves instead of trusting Christ)
- o   Denial (conscious or subconscious)
- o   Fantasy (escape from the real world)
- o   Emotional insulation (withdraw to avoid rejection)
- o   Regression (reverting back to a less threatening time in the past)
- o   Displacement (taking out frustrations on others)
- o   Projection (blaming others or accusing others of things we ourselves have done)
- o   Rationalization (defending self though verbal excursion)

To counter these and other deceptions we tell ourselves we need to exercise faith. Faith is the response to Truth and believing the truth is a CHOICE (not a feeling). If we say, "I want to believe God, but I just can't," then we are deceiving ourselves. Of course, we can believe God. We know that God does not lie. Faith is something we DECIDE to do; it is not something we FEEL like doing. Believing the truth does not make it true; rather it is TRUE, therefore we believe it.

Examine yourself and how you may deceive yourself with "self-deceptions" and "Self-Defense" mechanisms. The pray the following prayer: ...

Prayer to Know the Truth:

Dear Heavenly Father. I know that You desire truth in the inner self and that facing this truth is the way of liberation (John 8:32). I acknowledge that I have been deceived by the father of lies (John 8:44) and that I have deceived myself (1 John 1:8). I pray in the name of the Lord Jesus Christ, and since by faith I have received You into my life and am now seated with Christ in the heavenliest (Eph 2:6), I ask you Father to command all deceiving spirits to depart from me. I now ask You to *"search me, O God, and know my heart: try me and know my anxious thoughts; and see if there be any hurtful way in me, and lead me in the everlasting way"* (Ps. 139:23, 24) In the name of Christ Jesus I pray. Amen.

Knowing the truth about oneself, overcoming self-deceptions and the mechanism of self-defense that hide who we really are, includes understanding our faith in Christ. It is by Christ that our lives have meaning and substance.

The following prayer is the substance of that faith:

Affirmations

I believe that I am a child of God (1 Jn. 3:1-3) and that I am seated with Christ in the heavenlies (Eph. 2:6). I believe that I was saved by the grace of God through faith that is a gift and not the result of my own efforts or merits (Eph 2:8).

I choose to be strong in the Lord and in the strength of His might (Eph 6:10). I put no confidence in the flesh (Phil 3:3) for the weapons of warfare are not of the flesh (2 Cor. 10:4). I put on the whole armor of God (Eph. 6:10-20), and I resolve to stand firm in my faith and to resist the evil one.

I believe that Jesus Christ has all authority in heaven and on earth (Matt 28:18) and that He is the head over all rule and authority (Col 2:10). I believe that Satan and his demons and wicked spirits are subject to the Lord Jesus Christ and therefore to me in Christ since I am a member of Christ's body (Eph 1:19-23).

I believe that apart from Christ I can do nothing (John 15:5) so I declare my dependence upon Him.

I choose to abide in Christ in order to bear much fruit and to glorify the Lord (Jn 15:8) and to accomplish the work of sanctification that Christ began in me through the Cross (James 2).

I believe that since I am a member go God's royal family I have the authority, in the name of Christ Jesus, to ask the Father to command the devil to leave my presence, as I obey the command to resist the devil (James 4:7).

I reject any counterfeit gifts or works of Satan and his minions in my life.

I believe that the truth will set me free (John 8:32) and that walking in the light is the only path of fellowship and freedom (1 John 1:7). Therefore, as a royal member of God's household, I stand against Satan's deceptions by affirming all the doctrines of the Faith and by taking every thought captive in obedience to Christ (2 Cor 10:5).

I declare that the Bible and the Church are the only authoritative standards for me (2 Tim 3:15, 16).

I choose to speak the truth in love (Eph 4:15).

I choose to present my body as an instrument of righteousness, a living and holy sacrifice, and thus I renew my mind daily by the living Word of God in order that I may prove that the will of God is good, acceptable, and perfect (Rom 6:13; 12:1, 2).

I ask my heavenly Father to fill me with His Holy Spirit (Eph 5:18), to lead me into all truth (John 16:13), and to empower my life that I may live above sin and not carry out the desires of the flesh (Gal 5:16). I crucify the flesh (Gal 5:24) and choose to walk by the Spirit.

In making all these affirmations, I renounce all selfish goals and choose the ultimate goal of love (1 Tim 1:5). I choose to obey the greatest commandment to love the Lord my God will all my heart, soul, and mind, and to love my neighbor as myself (Matt 22:37-39). Amen.

Step 6 — Worship, Pray, and Fast

Worship as a Church Family: One of Satan's favorite lies, apart from having us believe that he does not exist, or that he does exist and is more powerful than he truly is, is that since God is everywhere and we can worship Him anywhere and do not need the "community of believers ", the Church family.

Although it is true that God is everywhere and worshiping Him anywhere is wholesome and good, it is false to believe that the Church is unnecessary. Since the earliest days of Christianity, communities of believers gathered together on the *Lord's Day* (Sunday).

Scripture is very clear on the subject of Church attendance and on how our submission to its authority is not only good but required. The Church, its leaders and members, are the Mystical Body of Christ here on Earth. To disobey the teachings of the Church as it relates to faith and morals is to disobey the teachings of Christ. To not attend church is also disobedience to Christ.

Paul admonishes those who do not come to Church in Hebrews 10:19-25:

Therefore, brothers, since through the blood of Jesus we have confidence of entrance into the sanctuary by the new and living way he opened for us through the veil, that is, his flesh, and since we have "a great priest over the house of God," let us approach with a sincere heart and in absolute trust, with our hearts sprinkled clean from an evil conscience and our bodies washed in pure water. Let us hold unwaveringly to our confession that gives us hope, for he who made the promise is trustworthy. We must consider how to rouse one another to love and good works. We should not stay away from our assembly, as is the custom of some, but encourage one another, and this all the more as you see the day drawing near.

Hebrews 13:17

Obey your leaders and submit to them; for they are keeping watch over your souls, as men who will have to give account. Let them do this joyfully, and not sadly, for that would be of no advantage to you.

Worship and prayer together as a family, prayer meetings, adoration, and other corporate settings, and in the privacy of the family at home is critical in developing spiritual health for the family and each family member. Such family devotion forms the foundation for all that each family does away from home in the world of school, work, and society.

Prayer is so important both in the family context and individually. It is important not just because prayer is something a Christian ought to do, but because prayer is communication.

The more we depend on God, the closer He is to us and we are to Him. Aligning ourselves with God, communicating with Him at all times and in all situations and personal decisions will unite our hearts to His. A heart united to the Creator will overflow with graces and blessings.

Prayer and Spiritual Warfare: In addition, a healthy prayer life destroys strongholds that demons may have in our lives and in our hearts. Without prayer we cannot hope to be delivered from spiritual afflictions. It is no secret —prayer, worship, devotion, and living the Christ-Life in all that it entails is the formula not only for deliverance from spiritual afflictions, but for living the victorious life in Christ.

When dealing with spiritual afflictions, however, some special prayer considerations may be needed. Scripture states that there are certain demons that will only respond to prayer as well as fasting: *"But this kind does not go out except by prayer and fasting."* (Matthew 17:21). If fasting can defeat even the strongest of fallen angels, just how powerful is this sacrifice that we can make?

Spiritual warfare prayers are very effective in defeating the enemy and drawing our hearts closer to God.

Step 7 — Live the Faith and Remain Faithful

Along with all the advice and recommendations of the first six steps, our healing and deliverance cannot be complete unless we act upon our faith. Doing good works and charitable acts of love are a natural outflow of our faith and necessary to lead a good Christian life. It is not enough to believe. James asks and admonishes in James 2:19,20, 26:

Do you still think it's enough just to believe that there is one God? Well, even the demons believe this, and they tremble in terror! Fool! When will you ever learn that faith that does not result in good deeds is useless?

Just as the body is dead without a spirit, so also faith is dead without good deeds.

James calls a man a fool who does not act upon his faith in James 1:22-25:

Be doers of the word and not hearers only, deluding yourselves. For if anyone is a hearer of the Word and not a doer, he is like a man who looks at his own face in a mirror. He sees himself, then goes off and promptly forgets what he looks like. But the one who peers into the prefect law of freedom and perseveres, and is not a hearer who forgets but a doer who acts, such a one shall be blessed in what he does.

It is hard to live the Christ-Life, but we must try. We must not have a faith that is dead and useless. We must not be a fool and not practice our faith. We must, rather, live out our faith and persevere in the faith:

1 Corinthians 9:23-27

All this I do for the sake of the gospel, so that I too may have a share in it. Do you not know that the runners in the stadium all run in the race, but only one wins the prize? Run so as to win. Every athlete exercises discipline in every way. They do it to win a perishable crown, but we an imperishable one. Thus, I do not run aimlessly; I do not fight as if I were shadowboxing. No, I drive my body and train it, for fear that, after having preached to others, I myself should be disqualified.

Colossians 1:17-23

He is before all things, and in him all things hold together. He is the head of the body, the church. He is the beginning, the firstborn from the dead, that in all things he himself might be preeminent. For in him all the fullness was pleased to dwell, and through him to reconcile all things for him, making peace by the blood of his cross (through him), whether those on earth or those in heaven.

And you who once were alienated and hostile in mind because of evil deeds he has now reconciled in his fleshly body through his death, to present you holy, without blemish, and irreproachable before him, provided that you persevere in the faith, firmly grounded, stable, and not shifting from the hope of the gospel that you heard, which has been preached to every creature under heaven, of which I, Paul, am a minister.

And thus, let us be able to say, with St. Paul, in 2 Timothy 4:6-8

For I am already on the point of being sacrificed; the time of my departure has come. I have fought the good fight, I have finished the race, I have kept the faith. Henceforth there is laid up for me the crown of righteousness, which the Lord, the righteous judge, will award to me on that Day, and not only to me but also to all who have loved His appearing.

Persevere in the faith and let your life be a living Gospel for you shall thereby *"know the truth and the truth shall set you free"*

I have outlined steps detailing certain issues that we have found important in gaining freedom for a person in spiritual affliction.

1. purify one's conscience by a good confession;
2. Receive Holy Communion as often as possible;
3. Implore the mercy of God by prayer and fasting.
4. Recourse to specific spiritual warfare prayers applicable to the situation.

Final Thoughts

Repentance, forgiveness, acting on our faith, praying, fasting, receiving the Sacrament frequently, and all the rest we ought to do as good Christians are very good things and very necessary for this life, but more importantly for the life to come.

The advice contained in these Steps to Self-Deliverance, however, are not "quick fixes". This advice involves a lifelong commitment for anyone with spiritual afflictions. Freeing yourself from the bondages of the enemy and keeping them from returning requires this commitment to persevere in Christ and in the Christ-life.

There will be dry times. Your faith will be tested. Indeed, the demons may (and more than likely will) try to return. Scripture speaks of what demons do once they are cast out:

Now when the unclean spirit goes out of a man, it passes through waterless places seeking rest, and does not find it. Then it says, 'I will return to my house from which I came'; and when it comes, it finds it unoccupied, swept, and put in order. Then it goes and takes along with it seven other spirits more wicked than itself, and they go in and live there; and the last state of that man becomes worse than the first. (Matthew 12, 43-45).

Do not leave your house (heart) *"unoccupied, swept and put in order"*; rather be filled with the Holy Spirit.

We can never let down our guard. As a final instruction, remember the teaching of St. Paul in Ephesians 6:10-18. We do not go about our day without putting on our clothes. Do not go into the world with God's armor:

Finally, draw your strength from the Lord and from his mighty power. Put on the armor of God so that you may be able to stand firm against the tactics of the devil. For our struggle is not with flesh and blood but with the principalities, with the powers, with the world rulers of this present darkness, with the evil spirits in the heavens. Therefore, put on the armor of God that you may be able to resist on the evil day and, having done everything, to hold your ground. So, stand fast with your loins girded in truth, clothed with righteousness as a breastplate, and your feet shod in readiness for the gospel of peace. In all circumstances, hold faith as a shield, to quench all (the) flaming arrows of the evil one. And take the helmet of salvation and the sword of the Spirit, which is the word of God. With all prayer and supplication, pray at every opportunity in the Spirit. To that end, be watchful with all perseverance and supplication.

APENDEX 1
Steps for Self-Deliverance

The purpose of all this information is to enable you to do a self-deliverance at home for yourself. The process of self-deliverance is carried out in stages. Let's go through them one by one.

STEP ONE: Start with praise and worship. You can sing songs to praise God and to worship Him.

STEP TWO: Confess out loud Scriptures promising deliverance. Luke 10:19, Ephesians 1:7, Romans 16:20, Revelation 12:11, Colossians 2:14-15, Galatians 3:13-14, Psalms 91:3…*2 Timothy 4:18* says And the Lord shall deliver me from every evil work, and will preserve me unto His heavenly kingdom: to whom be glory forever and ever. Amen. You should memorize *2 Tim 4:18*.

STEP THREE: Break covenants and curses to destroy their legal hold. You pray a simple prayer like this: I break any curse or covenant working against me, in the name of Jesus. (Simple prayers)

STEP FOUR: Bind all the spirits associated with those covenants and curses like this: I bind all the spirits attached or connected to the curses and covenants I have just broken, in the name of Jesus.

STEP FIVE: Lay one hand on your head and pray, Holy Ghost, cover me from the top of my head to the sole of my feet, in the name of Jesus. Begin to mention every organ of your body; kidney, liver, intestine, blood, etc. You must not rush at this level. Lay your hands-on areas that the Spirit of God leads you to.

STEP SIX: Then begin to saturate yourself with the Blood of Jesus. You do this by saying: I plead the Blood of Jesus over me. This must continue until you have a release in your spirit to stop.

STEP SEVEN: It is now, that you can demand firmly, in the name of the Lord Jesus Christ, that any spirit that is not of God should leave you. You demand it forcefully like this: In the name of the Lord Jesus Christ, I come against all you hidden spirits and I bind your activities in my life. You can no longer hide below the surface because I now recognize what you have been doing; release me, in the name of Jesus.

(If sickness is the problem, address it and say) You spirit of infirmity, I speak to you directly, get out of my life now. I am redeemed by the Blood of Jesus Christ, come out and go now. Go out with every breath by the power of the Holy Spirit. I prevail over you, in the name of Jesus.

__STEP EIGHT:__   Ask for a fresh in-filling of the Holy Spirit and close the session with praises. Self-deliverance keeps you from getting sick; it removes every evil seed of the enemy; it charges your body with fire. It uproots evil plantations and builds up your confidence. Every night before you go to bed, you must remember these two important prayer points.

1. Pray for cover with the Blood of Jesus. *__Revelation 12:11__* = And they overcame him by the Blood of the Lamb, and by the word of their testimony; and they loved not their lives unto the death.
2. Pray that the Angels of God should surround you. *__Psalms 34:7__* = The Angel of the Lord encampeth round about them that fear him, and delivereth them.

No matter how sleepy you are, make sure pray these two prayer points every night. There is no reason why self-deliverance should not be effective. However, if the person seeking deliverance is under stubborn demonic control or hereditary strongman and lacks sufficient faith or authority to defeat the oppressors or living in any known sin, the evil spirits will be hard to get rid of. right.

One final word of caution. For a person to be delivered, he/she must want deliverance. Self-deliverance must not be done because of pride, shyness, the fear of possible public embarrassment, etc. Your motive for engaging in self-deliverance has to be pure.

REMEMBER: *__DELIVERANCE IS A PROCESS (((NOT A ONE-TIME EVENT)))__* AND THE LENGTH OF TIME IT TAKES DEPENDS ON SEVERAL THINGS;

1. The length of time the spirit has stayed inside a person
2. The strength and reinforcement of the spirit
3. The experience and degree of anointing upon those who are ministering the deliverance
4. The willingness of the person being delivered to be free
5. The knowledge of the Word of God and your level of hatred for sin
6. SELF-DISCIPLINE IS NECESSARY

Also, remember that bondage can be weak or strong. A weak hold can be broken quickly, whereas a stronghold may take a more time. You will not realize the strength of bondage until you faithfully and persistently work on it. You must remember that a foothold can graduate to a stronghold if left unaddressed. After this exercise, set aside some days (with fasting). DO NOT CONTINUE TO DO THE THINGS THAT CAUSED THE "it"! CHANGE YOUR HABITS TO AGREE WITH YOUR PRAYERS. AMEN.

Appendix 2

Exposing the Doors to Bondage

Part I: The bondage

1. When did this bondage start?

2. Was there any unusual things that took place (or you did) when this bondage started?

3. If this bondage started when you were a child: Do you have ancestors who have suffered from a similar kind of bondage?

4. What kind of bondage are you facing? (Fears, depression, voices in your mind, mental illness, physical illness, mental torment, spiritual torment, etc... Please be as detailed as possible.)

5. What are all the things that have impacted your life? (Parent's death, trauma, a certain situation that changed your life, anything that 'changed' you.)

Part II: Your ancestor's background

1. Do you have ancestors who have struggled with similar problems or bondages?

2. Did your bondage start as a child and appear to have no reason to be there?

3. Do you have siblings who suffer from similar bondages or oppression?

Part III: Soul ties

1. Have you been involved with extramarital sex? Are you attracted to an ex-lover? Is he or she a good/godly influence for you?

2. Have you been divorced?

3. Do you feel an unusual attraction to a past boyfriend, girlfriend or lover (who is obviously not right for you)?

4. Do you let anybody dominate, control, or make your choices you?

5. Have you ever formed a blood covenant with another person? (Blood brothers, etc.)

6. Have you ever made vows or agreements with somebody in effort to strengthen the relationship or commit yourself to each other?

7. Do you see any ungodly relationships in your past where gifts were exchanged? (Are you holding onto something that was given to you from somebody you had adultery with, etc.)

8. Have you ever had ungodly relations with any one?

9. Do you have any pictures in your possession of somebody whom you may have an ungodly soul tie with? (A picture of you with somebody you had an adultery with, etc.)

Part IV: Relationship with parents

1. What do you think of your parents?

2. How would you explain your childhood?

3. Where you close to your parents while growing up? If not, why?

4. How would you explain your relationship with your parents? Was it good, bad or very cold?

5. Did you feel rejection from your parents?

6. Was either of your parents overly passive or controlling?

7. Has either of your parents been divorced? Remarried? Are your parents divorced?

8. How would you describe your relationship with your siblings growing up?

Part V: Rejection and abuse

1. Were your parents married when you were conceived? Were you the right sex? Did your parents not want you, or want you to be different (gender, etc.) in any way? If so, explain.

2. Did you feel rejected as a child? As an adult? If so, by whom? Explain.

3. Did you face abuse? What kind (emotional, physical, sexual, etc.) and by whom?

4. Have you faced rejection from your peers, classmates, friends or those around you?

5. Have you ever been put down, belittled, or made fun of? If so, by whom? Explain.

6. If you have faced rejection or abuse, how did you respond? Do you feel you are still paying a price for it? If so, how?

7. How do you respond to rejection right now?

8. Do you reject yourself (self-rejection)? If so, why and in what ways?

Part VI: Unforgiveness or bitterness

1. Is there anybody you feel edgy around? (Don't like them, feel anything in your heart against them, etc.)

2. Do you have anything against anybody? In other words, is there anybody that you have a hard time demonstrating the love of Christ to?

3. Has anybody wronged you that you haven't forgiven from your heart (thoughts, feelings, emotions, etc.)?

4. How do your view your siblings, parents, coworkers, etc.? Do you have any hard feelings against them?

5. Do you make a habit of blaming yourself for everything? Do you obsess over your mistakes and feel unusually guilty for them?

6. Do you deeply regret things that you've done in your past? Could you kick yourself over something you've done in your past? If so, explain.

Part VII: Personality

1. Are you a very positive or negative person?

2. Do you feel confident in yourself? If so, why?

3. Do you have a low self-esteem? If so, why?

4. Are you domineering or controlling? If so, to whom, and in what ways? Why?

5. Are you an achiever? (A go-getter) If so, in what ways?

6. Do you feel that you are always right and that if everybody did everything your way, this world would be a better place to live?

7. How do you treat your children? Husband? Are you controlling, passive, etc.?

8. Do you like people to 'look at you' (as in receive attention)?

Part VIII: Emotional health

1. Do you strive to feel accepted? If so, how does this affect your lifestyle? By whom do you want to feel accepted?

2. Are you always stressed out? If so, why?

3. Do you feel hurt? If so, by whom/what and why?

4. Do you feel good about yourself? If not, why?

5. Do you feel depressed? If so, why? When did it start? Did your parents or grandparents struggle with depression? If so, then do you know when it started and why? Do you have siblings who are also struggling? Do you feel your depression is rational or irrational?

6. Do you struggle with fears? If so, what is it that you fear? (Fear of heights, dying, being hopeless, failure, never marrying, etc.)

7. Do you worry about things? What things do you worry about? Why?

8. Do you struggle with anger? Do you have a short temper?

9. Do you have any insecurity? If so, explain.

10. Do you feel any self-pity or feel sorry for yourself? Have you ever felt this? If so, why?

11. Do you find it easy to hate people? If so, over what kinds of things would a person have to do to make you hate them?

12. Do you have any irrational feelings? If so, what are they?

13. Do you feel like something is wrong with you?

14. Do you feel excessively guilty over anything? Is this a continual problem?

15. Are you very confused and forgetful? (Beyond the normal)

16. Are you aware of any emotional wounds that have affected you?

17. Have you ever been deeply embarrassed over something? What was it?

18. Have you been in or are currently experiencing very difficult (depressing) circumstances which may cause you to feel hopeless or depressed?

Part IX: Who are you in Christ? And how do you see God?

1. How do you explain your relationship with God?

2. Do you feel you aren't good enough to meet His standards?

3. Do you see Him as a loving father, or a dictator?

4. Do you believe that it's only by the Blood of Jesus that your sins are forgiven? Or do you feel you need to earn your forgiveness in any way?

5. Do you feel God's love in your life?

6. Do you feel like your sins are forgiven? Or do you feel guilty?

7. Do you feel excessively guilty in everyday life?

8. Do you feel that doing good things, you earn God's love and acceptance?

9. Do you feel that God is angry or upset with you?

Part X: Spoken curses, vows & oaths

1. Have you ever spoken something negative about yourself that has come to past? For example: "I'm sick and tired..." or "If I don't quit typing, I'm going to get arthritis!"

2. Has your parents, or those in authority over you spoken out a curse over you? For example: "You'll never amount to anything!" or "You'll never get out of debt" or "You're so dumb"

3. Have you ever made a vow out of anger? If so, what? For example: "I'll never let anybody push me around again!" or "I'm never going to be hurt again!"

4. Have you ever wished to die? Have you ever said it?

5. If you have made any vows or oaths, what are they?

Part XI: Relationships

1. Do you have many friends? What kind of people are they?

2. Do you have a hard time trying to meet new people or make friends?

3. Are you socially outgoing or shy? If so, why?

4. How would you define your relationship with your spouse?

Part XII: Sexuality

1. Have you ever had unholy sex? What kind? (Fornication, adultery, sodomy, with a child, etc.)

2. Have you struggled with lust, fantasy or unholy sexual thoughts? If so, what kind?

3. Have you been attracted to pornography?

4. Do you have homosexual thoughts and desires? If so, have you acted upon those feelings?

5. How do you feel about your sexuality? (Do you feel dirty about it, or do you feel it's a wonderful blessing that God's given you?)

6. Do you withhold sex from your spouse or are you fidgety? Do you enjoy a healthy relationship with your spouse sexually? How does he or she react?

7. Have you ever been raped or sexually abused?

8. Have you ever woke up and felt a sexual presence with you? There are demons that imitate male and female functions, and stimulate their host (a person) sexually (beyond the normal 'wet dream').

9. Do you struggle or have you struggled with masturbation?

10. Do you struggle or have you struggled with any other sexual related thoughts, desires, or bondages?

11. Is there anything sexually that you are ashamed of?

Part XIII: Addictions

1. Do you have any addictions? If so, what kind? (Drugs, alcohol, smoking, eating, sex, TV, etc.) When did they start?

2. Did anybody else in your family (siblings, ancestors, etc.) have a struggle with any addictions? If so, what? Who?

3. Have you ever had, or currently have any sort of obsession over anything? If so, what?

Part XIV: False religions

Examples of false religions: Buddhism, Hindu, Jehovah Witness, Mormonism, Christian Scientists, eastern religions, etc.

1. Have you ever been involved with any false religions? If so, why, when and how long? How do you feel about those beliefs now?

2. Have you ever been involved in any secret societies such as Freemasonry? If so, how deep were you involved?

Part XV: The occult

1. Have you ever shown interest in the occult? If so, in what ways? (Read up on it, dabbled in it, etc.)

2. Do you still feel drawn or attracted to the occult?

3. Have you had any interest in horror or thriller style movies or novels? Are you still attracted to these things?

4. Have you ever made a vow with the devil? If so, what?

5. Married Satan?

6. Worshipped a demon or Satan?

7. Have you ever put a curse or spell on somebody?

8. Are you aware of any curses or spells placed on you? If so, what? Who did it?

9. Dabbled with an Ouija board? If so, why?

10. Ever been a member of a coven (group of 13 witches)? Explain.

11. Communicated with the dead? Explain.

12. Told somebody's fortune or went to see a fortune teller? Explain.

13. Ever read your horoscope?

14. Watched or been involved in a séance? Explain.

15. Have you been involved or a victim of Satanic Ritual Abuse (SRA)? Explain.

16. Been baptized into a false religion or any other evil baptism? If so, what were you baptized into? When?

17. Have you ever had a spirit guide?

18. Have you ever been involved with meditation, yoga, karate, or related activities?

19. Were you or anybody in your family superstitious? If so, who?

20. Ever been involved in astral travel? (Out of body)

21. If you have made any vows or oaths, what are they? Were there any sacrifices or rituals that were accompanied with them?

22. Have you ever made a blood pact before? If so, with whom (including persons, demons and Satan) and for what purpose?

23. Have you ever partaken in automatic writing, automatic drawing or automatic painting?

24. Have you ever been involved in Yoga, transcendental meditation, or similar activities?

25. Have you ever sought healing from a spiritual source other than Jesus Christ? (New age healing, energy healing, etc.)

26. Any other involvement in the occult? Explain.

Part XVI: Un-confessed sins

1. Are there any un-confessed sins that you have not repented of? (Usually something you've done, that you know is wrong, but won't admit to it. An abortion, stealing, etc. are some examples.)

2. Is there anything you've been hiding inside that you haven't confessed?

3. Do you feel excessively guilty over something(s) you've done in the past? If so, what?

Part XVII: Cursed objects

1. Do you have any idols, occult rings, or anything that could hold evil spiritual value in your home? If so, what? Any objects that hold evil spiritual value must be destroyed.

2. Do you have any gifts saved from sinful relationships? If so, explain. For example, if a man gives a woman a personal gift during an adultery that needs to be sold or destroyed.

Part XVIII: Severe trauma, abuse & disassociation

1. Have you ever been exposed to extreme abuse or a traumatic experience? Did it have a drastic effect on your emotional or mental system? If so, what happen? How did it affect you?

2. Have you ever disassociated or been diagnosed with Dissociative Identity Disorder (DID) or Multiple Personality Disorder (MPD)?

3. Are you aware of any alters (other personalities) that you may have? (If so, tell me about them)

4. Do you have a memory gap where you cannot remember a certain time of your life?

5. Do you have false memories of things that really didn't take place?

6. Have you ever been in a car accident or other traumatic situation? Have you ever witnessed a tragedy in real life?

Part XIX: Weaknesses

1. Do you struggle with any habitual sins? If so, what? Do you want to break those bad habits?

2. Do you struggle with any weaknesses such as lust, anger, hate, etc.? If so, what? Do you know where they came from or how they got started? Do you want to break free from those weaknesses?

Part XX: Pregnancy issues

1. Have you ever said something along the lines of, "I will never have children"?

2. Have you ever had an abortion or attempted one?

3. Have you ever had incest or ungodly sexual relations with somebody related to you? (See Leviticus 20:19-21, as this can cause a curse to land upon you which needs to be broken)

Part XXI: Other things to look for

1. Have you ever tried drugs? If so, how much, and how did it affect you? Why did you try drugs?

2. Have you ever thought about or attempted suicide?

3. Do you have any physical or mental disabilities, diseases or illnesses? Explain.

4. Do you want, and are willing to be delivered? Are you willing to give up those demon spirits and maybe make some lifestyle changes in order to keep your deliverance?

5. Do you experience unusual confusion settle upon you as you try to pray and read the Bible?

6. What kind of music do you like? (Please list all styles of music you currently enjoy, and give examples in each category you list, such as some names of artists and songs)

7. Have you previously enjoyed hard rock, metal, acid, alternative, rap, new age, or any other kind of worldly music? (Please provide some examples of artists and songs from each genre (type/style) of music you list)

8. Have you had any nightmares or weird experiences at night while supposedly sleeping?

9. Have you ever been in a trance or had an out of body experience?

10. Have you ever noticed time slipped right out from under you? For example, you look at your watch and its 7:00pm, then you look again what seemed like 15 minutes later and its 2:00am. This is a sign of a trance.

11. Have you ever touched or kissed a dead body? If so, explain whom and why and what happened afterwards.

12. Do you feel that you somehow have to earn your forgiveness? Do you 'wonder' if your sins are truly forgiven -- all of them? Are you aware of any signs of legalism or religious spirits operating in your mind?

13. Do you have any physical infirmities, sickness or diseases? If so, please list them.

14. Are you on any medications? If so, please explain.

15. Are you entertained by movies or TV shows which glorify death, murder, pain or suffering of others? Please explain.

16. Have you ever had any other kind of weird encounter with the spiritual realm?

Use this information to expose the root cause of the "it".

REFERENCES

1. Gary R. Collins, *Christian Counseling: A Comprehensive Guide*, 3rd Addition, Revised and Updated, NavPress, Colorado Springs, Colorado. ISBN 1418503290
2. Beilby, J.K. & P.R. Eddy. *Understanding Spiritual Warfare: Four Views*. Grand Rapids, Michigan: Baker, 2012.
3. Boyd, G.A., *God at War: The Bible and Spiritual Conflict*. Downers Grove, Illinois: IVP, 1997.
4. Hiebert, P. "Spiritual Warfare and Worldview"
5. Stedman, R.C, *Spiritual Warfare: Winning the Daily Battle with Satan*. Portland, Oregon: Multnomah, 1975.
6. Pirolo, N., *Prepare for Battle: Basic Training in Spiritual Warfare*, San Diego, California: Emmaus Road, International, 1997.
7. Arnold, E. C., *3 Crucial Questions about Spiritual Warfare*, Grand Rapids, Michigan: Baker, 1997.1
8. Rita Bennett, You Can Be Emotionally Free, 1982 ISBN 978 0 88270 748 8
9. Rita Bennett, Emotionally Free, 1982, ISBN 0 86065 194 0 Publishers, PO Box 777,
10. Tonbridge, Kent TN 11 0ZS, England, 1997, reprinted 2004). ISBN 1-85240-110-9. (Available in the US through the Arsenal Bookstore, 11005 Voyager Parkway, Colorado Springs, CO 80921.)
11. John and Paula Sandford, Healing the Wounded Spirit (Victory House, 1985). ISBN 0-932081-14-2.
12. Norma Dearing, The Healing Touch (Chosen Books, 2002). ISBN 0-8007-9302-1. Charles Kraft, Deep Wounds, Deep Healing (Servant Pub., 1993). ISBN 0-89283-784-5.
13. Derek Prince, God's Remedy for Rejection (Whitaker House, 1993). ISBN 088368-864-6.
14. Francis and Judith MacNutt, Praying for Your Unborn Child (1989). ISBN 0-38523-2829. (Available from www.Christianhealingmin.org, 904-765-3332.)
15. Thomas Verney, MD, The Secret Life of the Unborn Child (Summit Books, 1981).
16. Anderson, Winning Spiritual Warfare 1990 ISBN 13: 978-0-89081-868-8 James
17. Friesen, Uncovering the Mystery of MPD, 1997 ISBN 1-56819-062-7
18. Diane Hawkins, Multiple Identities, 2009 ISBN 978-0-9708073-6-6,
19. Restoration in Christ Ministries, http://www.rcm-usa.org/index.htm
20. Francis MacNutt, Deliverance from Evil Spirits, 1995, 0-8007-9232-7, Chap 17, pp 223-235 (best introductory material)
21. Daniel Ryder, Breaking the Circle of SRA, 1992, 0-89638-258-3 (an excellent book by a Christian counselor)
22. Margaret Smith, Ritual Abuse, what it is, why it happens, how to help, 1993, 0-06-250214-X (in depth information about SRA and MPD)
23. The Christian Bible
24. The following associations focus on trauma and disassociation www.sidran.org, www.issd.org
25. Pentecost, J.D., *Your Adversary the Devil*. Grand Rapids, Michigan: Zondervan, 1969

About the Author
Dr. Paulette Douglas

Dr. Paulette Douglas truly epitomizes elegance in living a saved, sanctified and Holy life, set apart from the secular world! Dr. Douglas is an ordained minister with the Pentecostal Assemblies of the World, an anointed national and international Evangelist, teacher and preacher. Dr. Paulette Douglas is renowned for the ministry of exhortation to the Body of Christ through deliverance, inner healing, salvation and biblical counseling at seminars, prayer clinics, crusades and conferences. She has established three churches and assisted in establishing many other churches, ministries and colleges as she serves on the Body of Christ for Jesus. Dr. Douglas was baptized in the name of Jesus Christ and filled with the Holy Ghost in 1977. She was called to the ministry in 1981, taught bible study at Pacific Bell for nine years which established the Radiant Life in Christ Ministries. She was the founder and pastor of the Radiant Life in Christ Community Church in Baldwin Park, California for nearly four years. Dr. Douglas retired in 1996 with full benefits from AT&T after 26 years of service. God introduced Dr. Douglas to the LOVE and HERO of her life, Bishop Robert T. Douglas Sr. They were married, the ministries merged, and she became the First Lady of the Jacob's Ladder Family, the Women's Ministry Director, the Church Executive Administrator and the Dean of the California University of Theology. Dr. Robert and Paulette Douglas are the proud parents of three wonderful children, Shakinah, Robert Jr. and Sondra Imani. They are also blessed with two granddaughters, Demi and Rob'Ann (butter ball) four grandsons, Dylan, Dominick Terrell, the twins Canden and Caden. Seven Godchildren and twelve God -grandchildren. Dr. Douglas is a graduate from Fuller Theological Seminary, Pasadena, California, Pentecostal Bible College, Ministerial Training Institute of Inglewood, California and Aenon Bible College West Coast. She has a Bachelors degree in Biblical Studies, a Masters degree in Theology, a PhD in Theology, Administration and a PhD in Biblical Counseling. She has earned certificates from California Christian Leadership of Orange County in biblical counseling, Zoe Christian Leadership Training Institute, Church Growth International, Seoul Korea and School of World Missions and Evangelism, Los Angeles. Dr. Douglas is formerly the Dean/Professor of the Inglewood Ministerial Training Institute of Inglewood, the Inland Empire Ministerial Training Institute, the Tri-County Ministerial Training Institute (San Bernardino, Riverside and Los Angeles counties) and the Living Waters Bible College, Rialto California. Dr. Douglas is presently the Dean of Colleges and Professor for the California District Council Aenon Bible College and Institutes, the Jacob's Ladder California University of Theology and Aenon Bible Institute CDC Extension Campus in Inglewood, California and the American College Theological Seminary International University (ACTS). All schools are fully accredited institutions for pastors, evangelist, teachers and anyone who has the call of God on their lives for ministry. Dr. Douglas is currently the CDC International Missions President and the past Church/Extension/Evangelism/Altar Director for the California District Council of the Pentecostal Assemblies of the World, Inc. Past Evangelism President for the CHDC Area 2 and has worked with the PAW Evangelism Ministry for more than 35 years. Dr. Paulette Douglas is the published author of the book series "Get Rid of It before It Gets Rid of You". Self-Help Instructions on how to correct and receive deliverance in every area of your life. Dr. Douglas portrays tremendous strength and endurance in the Lord by jointly sharing the vision and love for God with Bishop Douglas. Her primary objective in life is to be that "Excellent Woman of God, walking in His Divine favor.

Books and Recourses Compiled by
Dr. Paulette Douglas

"How to Get Rid of "it", Before "it" Gets Rid of You" Series (12 Books on Self Deliverance)

Volume One- Healing and Deliverance from Addictions

Volume Two- Healing and Deliverance from Sexual Addictions

Volume Three- Healing and Deliverance from Personality Disorders

Volume Four- Healing and Deliverance from Negative Relationships

Volume Five- Healing and Deliverance Through Spiritual Warfare

Volume Six- Healing and Deliverance from Negatives Attitudes

Volume Seven- Healing and Deliverance from Success Hindrances

Volume Eight- Healing and Deliverance from Tormenting Emotions

Volume Nine- Healing and Deliverance from Spiritual Weakness

Volume Ten- Healing and Deliverance from Salvation Issues

Volume Eleven- Healing and Deliverance from Domestic Problems

Volume Twelve- Healing and Deliverance Through Biblical Counseling

How to Have an Anointed Altar Workers Ministry

How to Have an Effective Prayer and Fasting Life

How to Walk in Your Grace as the Wife of a Minister, Deacon, Pastor, or Bishop

How to be an Effective Life Coach